CORE BUSINESS PROGRAM

MANAGEMENT ACCOUNTING

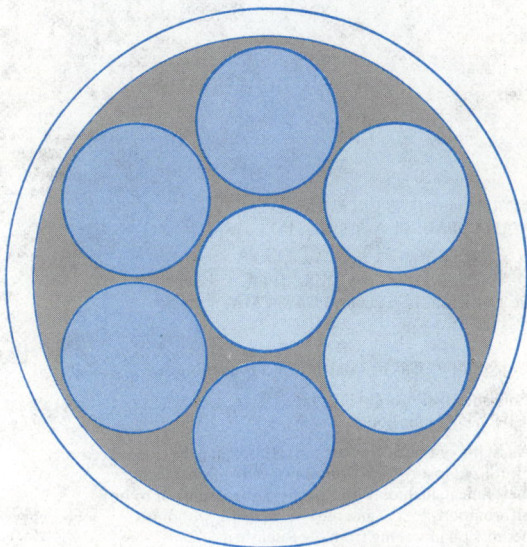

By
P. Fairfield
D. A. Harvey
M. Nettleton

Facts On File Publications
460 Park Avenue South
New York, N.Y. 10016

CORE BUSINESS PROGRAM
MANAGEMENT ACCOUNTING

P. Fairfield
D.A. Harvey, BSc(Econ), MSc, IPFA
M. Nettleton, BSc(Econ), FCA, FCMA,
FCIS, FBIM

First edition published in the United Kingdom in 1983 by
Mitchell Beazley London Ltd., Mill House,
87-89 Shaftesbury Avenue, London W1V 7AD, England.

Library of Congress Cataloging in Publications Data

Fairfield, Patti.
Management accounting.

1. Managerial Accounting. I. Harvey, D.A.   joint
author.
II. Nettleton, M.   joint author.
III. Title.
HF5635.F175 1985   658.1′511   84-8064
ISBN 0-8160-0050-6

Printed and Bound in Great Britain
1 0 9 8 7 6 5 4 3 2 1

Contents

Introduction

Management accounting is concerned with the provision of quantitative financial information to management for purposes of decision-making and control. Given the multitude of decisions which may need to be made within an organization, it should be apparent that the management accounting function is open-ended, and the management accountant must be able to respond in a constructive manner to any issues which arise. Despite the diversity in applications, a number of points may be made which are characteristic of management accounting issues in all organizations.

1. Decisions are based on information. Management accounting is particularly concerned with the collection of data on costs and profits and their analysis into appropriate formats to assist decision-making.

2. Decisions made should reflect the best use of the resources available. Management accounting is concerned with decision-making techniques for allocating resources in the most efficient manner from both short- and long-range planning perspectives.

3. Management must be certain that its decisions are being carried out efficiently and in accordance with its instructions, i.e. it needs to exercise control over the organization. Management accounting plays a significant role in the design and use of management control systems.

These key areas provide the rationale for the first ten chapters of the book, which emphasize:

1. Cost recording, classification and analysis.
2. Planning and control mechanisms.
3. Techniques for use in decision-making.

In carrying out his function, the management accountant will need to make frequent reference to financial reports, since published financial reports are a source of much useful information for decision-making. The final two chapters concentrate on those areas of financial accounting which are likely to impinge most closely on the work of the management accountant. They thus include a brief overview of financial accounts and a more detailed treatment of the analysis and interpretation of such accounts. Analysis of the performance of other organizations (based on information of the above type) can be invaluable to the management accountant in a number of ways, not least as a basis of comparison for performance appraisal purposes.

The overall aim of this book is to provide a broad coverage of the major areas of accounting of significance to management for purposes of decision-making and control. It should thus serve as an introduction to the study of management accounting as well as provide a basic reference source for management accounting concepts and techniques.

Chapter 1

The Role of Cost Accounting in Management Decision Making

Business firms consume economic resources to achieve economic ends. These economic resources can include raw materials such as mineral deposits, partially processed materials, the labor of individuals or machines used in the production process, and interest paid on the use of capital. The economic purpose of a firm is to make a profit on the goods and services produced. Those economic resources which are consumed in the process and which can be measured are recorded as **costs** to the firm. The difference between its costs and revenues is the firm's profit. Cost accounting encompasses the procedures that are needed to measure and record costs as well as those concepts and techniques that enable managers to use recorded information to maximize profits.

Cost accounting is the formalization of practices which are rooted in common-sense solutions to economic problems. More than the rote learning of formulas or procedures, the student's emphasis should be on becoming familiar with the type of questions experienced managers ask and understanding the factors which will determine the answers to those questions. The concepts and techniques introduced in this book will be generalizable to many problems encountered in the operation of a business organization, and should provide a solid foundation for future study.

The basic activities which comprise cost accounting may be summarized as follows:

1. Identification and measurement of costs incurred in pursuing specific objectives;

2. Analysis and classification of costs according to their behavior with respect to some variable of interest;

3. Recording of costs and reporting of costs in a form useful for management decision making;

4. Interpretation and use of cost data for planning and control of the firm's activities.

IDENTIFICATION AND MEASUREMENT OF COST

Identification and measurement of the costs incurred in providing economic benefits requires specification of the method by which costs will be accumulated. Two different methods (called costing systems) are generally used – **job order costing** and **unit or process costing**. These methods differ from each other in the unit to which specific costs are attached. The method selected will be determined by the nature of the production system.

Job order costing

In job order costing, all costs are accumulated by the particular "job" and are recorded when incurred. For example, a manufacturer of custom-made furniture would use job order costing to assign manufacturing costs to each piece of furniture as and when those costs are incurred. Each piece of furniture would be considered a job for the purposes of costing. Notice that the method of costing (job order) is logically determined by the nature of the production. In this case the discrete and individual nature of the product enables easy identification of the unit to which costs should be attached. Another example of job order costing would be the recording of all costs to particular clients by a consulting firm. Again, notice that it is the uniqueness of clients and their easy identification as individuals which dictate the use of the job order costing system.

Process costing

Process costing is used when one product cannot be differentiated from another. It is the lack of differentiability, not discreteness, that forces the selection of process costing. If the furniture manufacturer above produced assembly-line furniture then he would probably use process costing. Under process costing all costs of producing a particular type of product (a product line) are aggregated and the average cost is calculated and attached to each unit of output. Process costing is used when the firm produces large quantities of homogeneous products.

Regardless of the costing system in use, in any good costing system the costs ultimately assigned to a product will include those that have been incurred specifically in manufacturing (such as materials costs). Also included are costs not directly related to manufacturing (the classic example of which is the CEO's salary) but which must be incurred, and without which the main activity of manufacturing could not be carried out. Because a value judgment must be made in deciding how much of these latter costs should be included in the cost of a particular product, it follows that there is rarely a **unique cost figure** for a given unit.

ANALYSIS AND CLASSIFICATION OF COSTS

Costs can be analyzed according to their source, type or behavior. Although these classifications are related, it is important that a distinction between them be made. The form of any cost analysis will depend on the decision maker's reason for undertaking the analysis.

Source of costs

Economic resources may be classified into land, labor and capital. Hence, a common classification of costs follows from the classification of economic resources. Thus we speak of materials cost, labor costs, and depreciation and interest costs. The analysis of costs into these categories is useful to management in analyzing the overall cost of its production process. Usually there is some degree of substitutability between factors of production: word processors may be purchased to replace typists, higher quality raw materials may be purchased to eliminate some processing costs and management can use the breakdown of costs by source to choose the combination which will minimize overall production cost.

Types of costs

As noted earlier, costs may or may not be traceable to a specific job. Consider, for example, the custom furniture firm. There will be some costs directly attributable to a piece of furniture. These might include design costs as well as the costs of the materials and labor used in its manufacture and identifiable as such. Such costs are termed **direct costs**. Direct costs are those costs that can be specifically identified with a particular job or product-line, and include direct materials and direct labor. The distinguishing characteristic of direct costs is that it is possible to attach them to specific jobs or product lines. These costs include direct materials, direct labor and other direct costs. For example, the interest cost of money borrowed specifically to buy a crane to be used in a specific project can be part of the direct costs of that project.

Indirect costs are usually grouped under the heading **overhead** and include indirect materials, indirect labor and any other non-specific cost. If the firm engages in the manufacture of more than one piece of furniture at any period, it will allocate to each job a share of those costs that are non-specific. For example, all furniture pieces might be constructed using common equipment, or all orders might be handled through a central administrative department. These costs cannot be traced to any specific job. Such costs are termed **indirect costs** and are generally grouped together under the common heading of overhead. In general, overhead includes costs which cannot be attached to any specific job, or costs in which the effort of tracing them to a particular job does not yield a commensurate benefit. For example, the cost of coal bought for a factory's furnaces cannot be identified with a particular product; it is a cost incurred to facilitate the production process as a whole and is therefore an indirect materials cost. Similarly, a factory manager's salary must be considered a cost that is indirect to any particular product of that factory.

In both types of costing systems (recall job order and process costing), the identification and measurement of direct costs are usually unambiguous. The **allocation** of indirect costs to each product line or job is more difficult and requires experience and judgment. It will be readily seen that two types of judgments are required to attach indirect costs to a unit of output. First a judgment has to be made as to which costs are to be considered indirect. The second decision involves specific allocation of indirect costs among the product lines or jobs.

Behavior of cost

Another useful method of classifying costs is by the relation that they bear to the decision variable of interest, normally the level of production cost. **Variable costs** are costs that vary in propotion to production level. There are other costs that do not vary with production level within a certain production range. These are called **fixed costs**. The important variable in fixed costs is time, given that production level ranges over the portion that maintains costs fixed. The statement that a cost is "fixed" presumes that the relevant parameters of the decision specify a time horizon of a given length and a given production range.

Costs sometimes contain both fixed and variable components, which are known as semi-variable costs. In any analysis in which costs are deemed to be semi-variable the fixed and variable components must be separated and analyzed as fixed and variable costs. For example, total telephone costs might be broken down into the rental charge which is fixed (given a certain fixed number of telephones) and the variable call charge which is dependent on the number of telephone calls made.

Costs may therefore be analyzed in three ways: by source, type or behavior. Of course, they could be analyzed by using an infinite number of other criteria, but these three are considered the most useful. As the student becomes more familiar with cost accounting techniques, the usefulness of these systems of analysis will become more apparent.

COST ACCUMULATION AND ALLOCATION

The accumulation of costs within a recording and reporting system is an important function. Such systems are often dictated by management's requirements, which can range from a need to motivate divisional managers to the necessities of physical location. The essential feature of a cost recording system is that it collects data from a large number of sources. The reporting system then processes this data to produce information which is relevant for management's decisions.

The cost recording system should be flexible enough to enable the reporting system to provide the reports required by management. For example, the internal cost accounting system for a brokerage firm might be expected to produce information on profitability by specific broker, by specific account, by transaction volume, or by type of security. A poorly designed system would be unable to produce this information in a timely and organized manner.

A cost reporting system must produce accounting reports that present information to individual managers in a manner that will aid them in their decision making. The major elements of a cost reporting system are budgets, standards and variance reports. **Budgets** represent a statement of management plans for the budgetary period and may be regarded as a summary statement of the firm's objectives.

Budgets are usually developed by using **standards** to estimate the selling prices and unit costs expected to prevail for the period covered by the budget. A price standard for the purchasing department would state how many dollars per unit of raw material the department was expected to pay. A raw material usage standard for the manufacturing department would specify the number of units (e.g. in pounds or gallons) of raw material that it was expected to use per unit of output. Standards are based on the long-run average performance of the firm operating under normal conditions. **Variance reports** highlight deviations from expected performance during the period covered by the report. Variance reports may be general or detailed, depending on the requirements of management. When prepared on a timely basis, the variance reports help management identify potential problem areas, such as an increase in the amount of raw material being used to produce a unit of output. Variance reports can also provide a basis for performance evaluation by showing the differential between anticipated and actual performance in different departments or divisions.

Accounting reports will not provide useful information for management unless costs are appropriately classified. Following is a summary of the more common forms of cost classification.

1. By object of expenditure: The most basic classification of costs is by object of expenditure, or resource consumed. Although this method of classification is likely to result in the greatest proliferation of accounts, it also results in an accounting system with the greatest degree of flexibility. Each account would contain only those costs for a specific resource, for example labor costs (perhaps further classified as regular and overtime), office supplies, or direct materials (again, possibly classified into accounts for each type of material consumed).

2. By organization unit: Firms are usually organized into various functional units, or departments, and costs can be classified in accordance with these departments. Functional departments might include production, sales, distribution, and administration. Thus, for example, all factory costs would be assigned to the production department, salesmen's travelling costs would be assigned to the sales department and the chief accountant's salary would be assigned to the administration department. These departments are then referred to as **responsibility centers**, reflecting the expectation that each department head will be held responsible for costs incurred by his department. A responsibility center may be subdivided into two or more cost centers if a finer breakdown of the costs is desired. For example, the production department, a responsibility center, could be subdivided into two cost centers: the assembly unit and packaging unit.

3. By end-product or activity: Costs can also be classified by the unit of output or activity for which purpose they were incurred. Most costs are ultimately assigned to some end-product or activity, for example the manufacturing of a product or its distribution. The two costing methods reviewed above, job order costing and process costing, represent the two techniques in use for classification by end product or activity.

The above methods of cost classification are not mutually exclusive and combinations of more than one method can be used. For example, costs may be classified by object of expenditure, as well as by department, as in Figure 1. The costs could also be aggregated by end product or activity, provided a record is kept of which costs are incurred for which purposes. The widespread use of computerized accounting systems makes the process of reclassifying costs by object of expenditure, organization unit, or end product relatively simple and thus a combination of these particular methods is often found in practice. The method, or combination of methods, of cost classification is selected by management on the basis of information requirements and the degree of complexity to be built into the cost accounting system. The cost classification system should be flexible enough to provide management with a basis for creating different cost figures for different decisions, while at the same time being no more complex than the information requirements of management warrant.

Object of expenditure	Department	
	100 Editorial	101 Production
01 Direct materials	100.01	101.01
02 Direct labor	100.02	101.02
03 Vacation pay	100.03	101.03
04 Travel expenses	100.04	101.04
05 Overtime	100.05	101.05

Figure 1. Account numbers for a two-dimensional classification system

INTERPRETATION AND USE OF COST DATA

As noted in the preceding section, a good cost reporting system provides information for the purposes of decision-making and control. Budgets, standards, and variance reports are essential features of any reporting system. However, these represent only the most general forms in which cost information may be presented. Management faces many specific decisions in carrying out operations for which specialized accounting reports can provide useful information. Examples of the kind of problems managers might face are:

1. The firm is considering launching a new product line. Given its assumptions about production and advertising cost as well as market size, how should the product's selling price be determined?

2. A cash shortage is forcing management to shut down one of its production facilities. What are the consequences of the various options and how should they be compared?

3. A strike by one of the firm's suppliers has made an essential material temporarily unavailable. The firm is in a position to convert one of its plants to produce the raw material. Alternatively, it may buy the material from a competitor. What impact will each option have on the firm's profits?

4. A customer has asked the firm to produce a special order of a custom-made product on a one-time basis. It is offering to pay 80% of the normal unit price. The firm has excess capacity in one of its factories. What factors should the firm consider in accepting the order?

5. An internal dispute has arisen within a consulting firm about the quality and turn-around time of its reproduction services. The manager of one department has asked permission to contract with an outside supplier for typing and copying work. How should this dispute be mediated?

Accounting reports may be prepared in such a way as to provide the necessary information for assessing the short-term consequences of management decisions in each of the situations above. Techniques for analyzing similar problems will be presented in this text. Caution must be observed, however, in interpreting any accounting report. First, the information contained therein is only as good as the original data and the initial assumptions made in its preparation. For example, a factory which expects to operate at 100% capacity and establishes accounting systems on that basis will need to reinterpret its accounting reports if it only operates at 60% capacity during the year. Second, management must be wary of basing decisions on the short-term consequences of its actions as reflected in accounting reports. Long-term strategic planning is equally important for good management, and sometimes requires that profitable options be sacrificed currently in order to maximize future profits.

With all costing systems it is important to bear in mind that, because of the cost of operating the system, the value of the information produced should be viewed in relation to the cost involved in providing it. Complicated and costly information which merely confuses the user is of little value to a firm. On the other hand clear, concise information, promptly produced, can help management control the company's affairs and make rational decisions concerning its short and long run options.

Chapter 2

Manufacturing Cost Flows and Total Absorption Costing

RECORDING MANUFACTURING COSTS

Although a distinction is usually made between **managerial**, or cost accounting, and **financial accounting** for external reporting purposes (the last two chapters of this book present a brief review of financial accounting), the same set of data is used for both purposes and the preparation of cost figures for use in external reporting is accomplished by the firm's internal reporting system. A basic understanding of the cost flows which underlie the firm's balance sheet and income statement is central to the study of managerial accounting. In this section we will trace the cost flows through the accounts used in a process costing system. The cash flows for a manufacturing company, in this case a firm which makes wooden toys, are outlined in Figure 2.

In the example, the factory has only one production department. This department is a **cost center**, meaning it is an organization segment for which costs are accumulated. All resources consumed there, direct as well as indirect costs, must be recorded in the appropriate accounts and charged to production. The production process is assumed to consist of three distinct stages:

1. The machining stage, which takes place in the machine shop.

2. The assembly stage, which takes place in the assembly area.

3. The paint spray stage, which takes place in the paint shop.

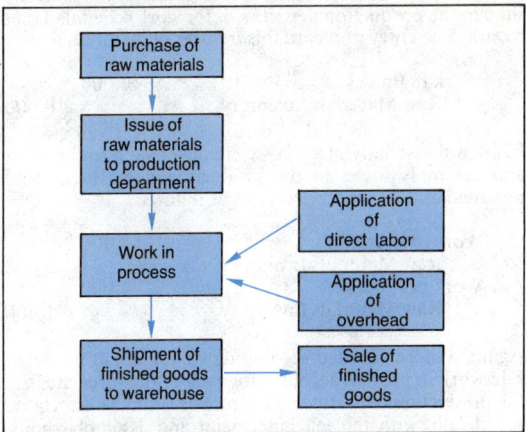

Figure 2. Cost flows for single product company

As production takes place, the internal accounting system will record the associated costs in specific accounts. To illustrate this process, we will trace the flow of manufacturing costs during the month of January for the firm described above using journal entries. A journal is a type of corporate diary, in which are recorded all economic transactions. Periodically information in the journal is summarized and **posted** to the accounts. For the sake of this illustration, we assume a perfectly efficient operation; that is, no materials are lost or spoiled, no labor hours are spent in anything other than manufacturing, and management can predict exactly the number of units of output to be produced each period. Few firms operate under such conditions, and the usefulness of the accounting system in analyzing the effects of departures from such efficiency will be discussed in Chapter 6.

On January 1, the firm purchases a quantity of raw materials, including $20,000 of lumber, $6,000 of paint, and $2,000 of nails, screws, and glue for cash. The entry to record these purchases is

Raw Materials Inventory	28,000	
Cash		28,000

The **debit** to the raw material inventory account represents an increase in that asset; the **credit** to cash represents a decrease in the amount of cash held. As noted in Chapter 1, when the raw material cost is recorded, it would probably be classified in two ways: it would be identified as raw material as well as a cost associated with the production department. A more detailed accounting system would have separate raw material accounts for the lumber, paint and assembly materials; to illustrate the principle at work, we use only one account.

The same day, $10,000 of lumber is issued to the machine shop in the production department for work scheduled that month. The entry to record this transfer of materials is

Work in Process	10,000	
Raw Materials Inventory		10,000

Paint and assembly materials were also issued to the paint and assembly areas in the production department, and recorded as direct materials costs as follows:

Work in Process	3,000	
Raw Materials Inventory		3,000
Work in Process	1,000	
Raw Materials Inventory		1,000

Again, a more detailed accounting system might use separate work in process accounts for each of the three areas in the production department. Then costs could be associated specifically with the machine, paint and assembly shops. This would have the effect of facilitating the analysis of product costs for the firm. For this example we will use only one work in process account.

The payroll for the entire production department was $15,000 for the month of January. The $15,000 is considered a direct labor cost, and is applied to Work in Process.

| Work in Process | 15,000 | |
| Salaries Payable | | 15,000 |

Rent on the factory building for the month was $2,000, and the electric bill was $1,000. These costs were assigned to an overhead account, as indirect production expenses.

| Factory Overhead | 3,000 | |
| Accounts Payable | | 3,000 |

The factory supervisor's salary for the month was $1,500.

| Factory Overhead | 1,500 | |
| Salaries Payable | | 1,500 |

One-twelfth of the company's $1,200 insurance policy expired, for which the premium had been paid at the beginning of the year.

| Factory Overhead | 100 | |
| Prepaid Insurance | | 100 |

Depreciation for the month on all machinery and equipment in the production department totalled $6,000.

| Factory Overhead | 6,000 | |
| Accumulated Depreciation | | 6,000 |

Because only one type of toy is being produced in the factory, all factory overhead must be assigned to that product line. The overhead account represents real costs which must be associated with some profit-making activity. In this case it is the manufacturing of wooden toys, so the costs are **allocated** to that product line.

This is accomplished with the following entry:

| Work in Process | 10,600 | |
| Factory Overhead | | 10,600 |

There was no work in process in the production department at the beginning of January, and none was left at the end of the month. One hundred thousand toys were transferred to the warehouse as finished goods on January 31.

| Finished Goods Inventory | 62,500 | |
| Work in Process | | 62,500 |

This illustrates the basic flow of costs through the firm, and the associated recording process. Direct manufacturing costs were assigned directly to a work in process account for a particular product; indirect costs were assigned to a temporary overhead account. The unit cost of each of these one hundred thousand toys produced in the above example may be calculated as $0.625. Of that cost, a little over ten and one-half cents ($10,600/$100,000) is attributable to overhead expenses.

THE PROBLEM OF PRODUCT COSTING

All **operating costs**, regardless of their initial classification by the accounting system, will ultimately be assigned to an end product or activity. All **manufacturing costs**, including overhead, will be assigned to a product, as shown in the example above. The costs associated with such ancillary activities as advertising or administration may be accumulated separately and not assigned to a product account. Accountants refer to the former as **product costs**, the latter as **period costs**. Product costs will be carried in inventory as work in process or finished goods, and expensed in the form of cost of goods sold in the period in which the items are sold. Period costs will be expensed directly on the income statement in the period in which the costs are incurred.

Product costing, that is the application of direct and indirect costs to units of output, is a simple process when only one product type is manufactured. All overhead costs are allocated to this product line, as in the example given above. Product costing, however, is more complicated when more than one product type is produced in a factory using a process costing system, or when a job costing system is in use.

Direct costs, those which may be traced directly to a specific production process, will simply be charged to specific jobs or contracts (under a job costing system), or the flow of production recorded over a specific period of time (under a process costing system), as was done above. Indirect costs, however, are not traceable to a particular job or production process. They relate to the running of the factory as a whole (as in the example, depreciation, insurance, and rent) rather than to any specific product unit, job, contract or flow of production. They are necessary to facilitate the production process, but are not costs that can be related directly to a particular production unit.

These indirect costs may be grouped together under the common heading overhead, as in the example above, and charged to production. When more than one product type is manufactured, a certain proportion of the total overhead cost will be assigned to each unit of output by means of an **overhead** rate. (The overhead rate is referred to by a number of different terms, of which the following are the most common: **overhead absorption rate, overhead allocation rate, standard overhead costs**, and **burden rate**.) The allocation of overhead expenses requires judgment in situations where more than one product is being manufactured. A method must be devised to determine how the overhead costs of the factory may be fairly allocated among the product units, jobs, contracts or production processes. The allocation of overhead is important from the point of view of management for two reasons:

1. Management will wish to determine the relationship between different production processes and the total costs of production, so that the most profitable use may be made of its resources. For example, a particular manufacturing process might be labor intensive, while another is capital intensive. For a firm which produces several different products, the choice between these methods may be affected by the allocation of the capital costs among product lines.

2. Management will wish to ensure that the selling price for each product has been fixed at a level that is in excess of the long run **total** costs that are being incurred in producing it. If more money could be saved by closing down a part of the factory than by producing and selling a particular product, then management would like its cost allocation system to signal that.

The method of allocation therefore should ensure that the amount of the overhead costs added to the direct costs of production fairly reflects that particular product's utilization of, and benefits from, the overhead costs. Furthermore, to provide meaningful and useful information on product costs to management, the method used should ensure that all factory overhead costs are allocated to product costs. In this way, the resultant product costs can each be said to contain an appropriate share of the total factory overhead costs, hence the term total absorption, or full, costing.

THE CHARGING OF FACTORY OVERHEAD TO PRODUCTION

The charging of factory overhead (also called production overhead) to production, in a case where more than one product is being manufactured, will be examined in detail. We will refer to the same company described above, only now we will assume that the company added two additional product lines in February, so that it now manufactures three types of toys: wooden blocks, mobiles, and soldiers. Below is the production data for February for all three product lines, including direct materials, direct labor, and the general factory expenses.

Production Department:	Blocks	Mobiles	Soldiers	Total
Direct materials				
Lumber	30,000	6,000	8,000	44,000
Paint	3,000	4,000	3,000	10,000
Assembly materials	1,000	1,500	1,000	3,500
Direct labor cost	15,000	12,000	20,000	47,000
Direct labor hours	2,500	1,875	2,500	6,875
Machine hours	4,000	2,000	2,000	8,000
Units produced	100,000	30,000	40,000	170,000
Factory Overhead:				
Supervision				1,500
Rent				2,000
Electricity				2,000
Depreciation				14,000
Insurance				100

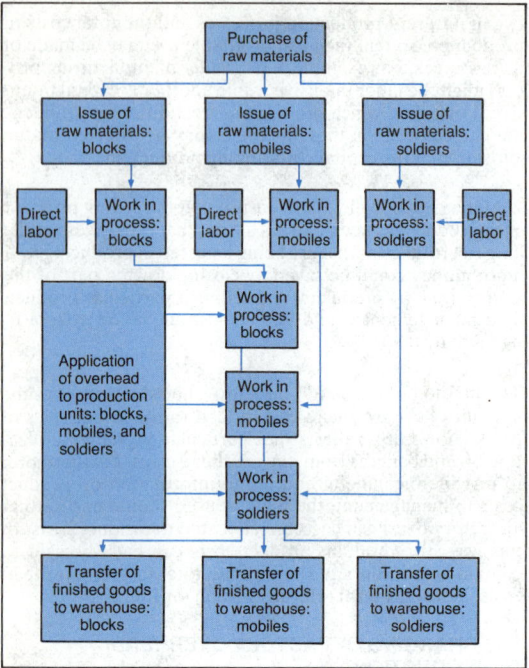

Figure 3. Cost flows for multi-product company

Figure 3 shows in diagrammatic form, the steps involved in charging costs to production. The costs of direct materials and direct labor are charged directly to the production. The factory overhead is divided among the three product lines and added to the work in process accounts for blocks, mobiles, and soldiers. Many different allocation bases may be used; the underlying process is the same. The following discussion will illustrate some of the more common overhead allocation methods, and will demonstrate the results when they are applied to the toy factory.

ILLUSTRATION OF OVERHEAD ALLOCATION USING DIFFERENT BASE UNITS

1. Product unit: Perhaps the most obvious basis of overhead allocation is the product unit. Using this method, the overhead absorption rate would be expressed in dollars per unit. The rate is found by dividing total overhead by the number of product units to be produced each period, to get an **overhead allocation rate (OAR)**. (This is the method used above to calculate an overhead cost of $0.106 per unit for the toys produced in January.) Applying this method to the data from our toy company in February, we would divide the total overhead cost of $19,600 by 170,000 units, to give us a per unit overhead cost of $0.115. The resulting unit costs for our toy company would be as follows:

	Blocks ($)	Mobiles ($)	Soldiers ($)
Direct materials	0.34	0.38	0.30
Direct labor	0.15	0.40	0.50
Overhead	0.115	0.115	0.115
Unit cost	0.605	0.895	0.915
Unit selling price	1.000	1.000	1.000
Gross margin before non-manufacturing expenses	0.395	0.105	0.085

The resulting overhead allocation rate does not, however, take into account the fact that the indirect resource demands of the products may be of very different magnitudes. That is, the manufacturing process of one unit of "Product A" may require two or three times the floor space or indirect labor time as one unit of "Product B," and accordingly, use more overhead. Applying the same amount of overhead to each product type does not satisfy any of management's objectives as set forth above; the resulting product costs will not reflect their relative overhead requirements, nor will the unit cost for each product line necessarily reflect its long run average cost. Thus, although simple, this method of applying overhead is rarely used in firms which produce more than one product type.

2. Direct labor hours: One of the more common bases used for overhead absorption is hours of direct labor (i.e., labor applied specifically to the production process). The overhead allocation rate is determined using the formula below:

$$OAR = \frac{\text{Factory overhead for period}}{\text{Total direct labor hours for same period}}$$

This method of charging overhead to production, on the basis of direct labor hours expended on the manufacturing, reflects the expectation that the greater the time expended on production, the greater the benefit derived from or use made of the factory overhead expenses. The overhead absorption rate for the toy factory is calculated in the following example:

$$OAR = \frac{\$19,600}{6,875 \text{ hours}} = \$2.85 \text{ per direct labor hour}$$

For each unit produced in February, the toy company would add $2.85 in overhead costs for each direct labor hour used in its production. For example, a block required 0.025 labor hours to produce, so $0.071 in overhead costs would be charged to it. The unit costs for the toy company using this overhead allocation method would be as follows:

	Blocks ($)	Mobiles ($)	Soldiers ($)
Direct materials	0.34	0.38	0.30
Direct labor	0.15	0.40	0.50
Overhead	0.071	0.178	0.178
Unit cost	0.561	0.958	0.978

Total production cost during the period, including overhead, would be allocated as follows (with total overhead cost slightly less than $19,600 due to rounding):

	Blocks ($)	Mobiles ($)	Soldiers ($)
Direct materials	34,000	11,500	12,000
Direct labor	15,000	12,000	20,000
Overhead	7,125	5,344	7,125

3. Direct labor dollars: Another method of charging overhead costs to production is to base the overhead allocation rate on the direct labor **cost** incurred. The rate would be calculated as follows:

$$OAR = \frac{\text{Factory overhead for period}}{\text{Total direct labor dollars for same period}}$$

$$OAR = \frac{\$19,600}{\$47,000} = \$0.417 \text{ per direct labor dollar}$$

The OAR will be identical to that calculated using direct labor hours as the base unit when the wage rate for workers making the products is the same. If, however, as is the case for the toy factory, one of the products requires more highly skilled (and therefore more expensive) labor than the others, the allocation of the overhead cost between them would differ under the direct labor hours and the direct labor dollars methods. The underlying assumption of this allocation method is that a product line's overhead requirements are more highly correlated with the costs of the labor used than with the number of hours of direct labor required.

For the toy factory, the product costs using this allocation are:

	Blocks ($)	Mobiles ($)	Soldiers ($)
Direct materials	0.34	0.38	0.30
Direct labor	0.15	0.40	0.50
Overhead	0.063	0.167	0.208
Unit cost	0.553	0.947	1.008

Note that under the latter method, increases in wage rates or productivity bonus payments during an accounting period can result in an additional charge for overhead being made to production, even where the level of overhead remains unchanged or productivity improvements reduce the production time.

4. Machine hours: A variant of the above method can be used in factories where the amount of machine time in relation to the amount of direct manual labor time is significant, for example in largely automated factories. In these circumstances a more rational base unit to use might be machine hours, the number of hours the machinery is in operation. An overhead allocation rate would be calculated as follows:

$$OAR = \frac{\text{Factory overhead for period}}{\text{Total machine hours for same period}}$$

The specific rate for the toy factory would be:

$$OAR = \frac{\$19,600}{8,000} = \$2.45 \text{ per machine hour}$$

For the toy factory, the resulting unit costs would be:

	Blocks ($)	Mobiles ($)	Soldiers ($)
Direct materials	0.34	0.38	0.30
Direct labor	0.15	0.40	0.50
Overhead	0.098	0.163	0.115
Unit cost	0.588	0.943	0.915

CHOOSING AN ALLOCATION BASIS

The overhead allocation methods illustrated above are among those most commonly used for product costing purposes. Many other possibilities exist; for example, rental costs could be assigned to production on the basis of relative floor space occupied by the associated machinery; insurance premiums could be allocated according to the value of the machines insured; fuel costs could be apportioned using a measure of energy consumed in the production process. The choice of an allocation basis is a matter of judgment and does not affect the actual cost incurred. The chart below shows the four different unit costs calculated for the toy company using the different allocation bases.

Allocation basis	Blocks ($)	Mobiles ($)	Soldiers ($)
Units	0.605	0.895	0.915
Direct labor hour	0.561	0.958	0.978
Direct labor dollar	0.553	0.947	1.008
Machine hour	0.588	0.943	0.915

In general, the basis to be used should be that which is most closely related to the actual incidence of overhead costs. When production data is available for only a short period of time, as is the case with the toy factory, it is difficult to determine the relationship between overhead costs and each of the possible bases for allocation. When more information is available, one simple way of choosing the best allocation basis is by plotting overhead costs against each of the possible bases, and choosing the one with the highest correlation. For example, assume we have the data on the toy factory for four months (during which time they added two additional product lines):

	January	February	March	April
Total overhead cost	$10,600	$19,600	$24,000	$26,000
Total direct labor hours	2,500	6,875	7,625	7,600
Total direct labor dollars	15,000	47,000	40,000	65,000
Total machine hours	4,000	8,000	9,800	10,600
Total units	100,000	170,000	180,000	250,000

If overhead costs are plotted on graph paper against each possible basis, or if an overhead allocation rate is calculated for each month under each of the possible methods, it will be observed that the most consistent rate over time is found by using machine hours as the basis. This exercise is left to the student.

In some cases, more than one method might be used in order to best reflect the relationship between overhead costs and output. For example, in the toy factory, one possible solution would be to use machine hours as the basis to allocate depreciation cost, and direct labor hours to allocate the other costs.

THE USE OF BUDGETED FIGURES

In the illustration above, the OAR was based on actual costs incurred in February, and the actual output. However, in most cases, product cost information will be required as soon as an accounting period commences. The only way to calculate a precise overhead absorption rate is to wait until the end of the accounting period, when the total overhead actually incurred is known and the actual production data is available. It is not realistic to do this in practice because it means a long delay between the start of production and the recording of product cost. The problem is solved by using an approximate figure for overhead absorption rates rather than waiting for a precise figure. The approximate figure is derived from budgeted figures for overhead costs and production output. Thus, for example, the overhead absorption rate might be calculated using budgeted factory overhead and the planned number of direct labor hours for the coming year.

To facilitate comparisons for control purposes, overhead absorption rates usually remain unaltered for a complete accounting year. Under these circumstances, it is unusual for the budgeted overhead and the expected output to be equal to the actual output in any period. Assume, for example, that a temporary shortage of raw materials led the toy factory to produce only 50,000 blocks in February, half as many as planned. Since the factory did not shut down, there was no corresponding reduction in overhead costs. Using direct labor hours as the basis for overhead recovery (yielding an OAR of $2.85 per direct labor hour), the total **allocated** costs for February would be:

	Blocks	Mobiles	Soldiers
Units	50,000	30,000	40,000
Direct materials	$17,000	$11,500	$12,000
Direct labor	7,500	12,000	20,000
Overhead (direct labor hours OAR of $2.85)	3,550	5,344	7,125
Total production cost	$28,050	$28,844	$39,125

Note that the total overhead absorbed is only $16,010, while the total overhead cost for the period was $19,600. The remaining amount is referred to as **under-absorbed** factory overhead. The reverse situation, the application of more overhead costs to units of output than were actually incurred, is called **over-absorption** of factory overhead.

TREATMENT OF UNDER- OR OVER-ABSORBED FACTORY OVERHEAD

If management's budgeted production data reflects attainable goals, the amount of overhead under- or over-absorbed in each period should be relatively small, and the amount of overhead absorbed during a year should approximate the budgeted amount. As long as this is the case, the treatment of this expense is of little consequence. It may be added to the cost of goods sold during the period, or added to the cost of goods in inventory, or divided between the two in proportion to the amounts of work completed and sold during the period.

TOTAL ABSORPTION COSTING IN PRACTICE

The number of cost centers set up within an accounting system will depend on the nature of the production and the level of cost information required by management. The method selected for the recovery, or charging of factory overhead for each production cost center, will be the method considered to be most suitable for that cost center. Thus different cost centers may well use different methods of overhead recovery. In a less elaborate accounting system, one overhead absorption rate might be calculated and used for the whole factory. In more complex accounting systems, factory overhead may be separated into fixed and variable elements and a separate overhead recovery rate calculated for each. This will enable a breakdown of fixed and variable overhead costs to be shown in the resulting accounting statements.

ACCOUNTING INFORMATION PROVIDED BY TOTAL ABSORPTION COSTING

Under total absorption costing, a reasonable total production cost for any specific product, job, contract or flow of production can be obtained at any stage of the production process. By applying the relevant overhead absorption method, a product cost can be obtained which includes an appropriate charge for overhead, to be added to the direct materials and direct labor costs. This can provide management with information as and when required to assist in the monitoring of both selling price levels and job, contract and production profitabilities.

For the firm as a whole, charges will also be made in the accounting statement at the end of each accounting period for selling, distribution and administrative overhead, plus any under- or over-recovery of production overhead. Sometimes selling and distribution overhead are added together.

The resulting accounting statement for the firm as a whole appears in the following format:

	($)	($)
Sales Revenue		180,000
Direct material	20,000	
Direct labor	35,000	
Production overhead	65,000	
		120,000
Gross Margin		60,000
Under-absorbed overhead		5,000
Selling and distribution overhead		25,000
Administrative overhead		15,000
Net profit		15,000

Full costing is a widely used cost recording technique. It is not, however, useful for many decision-making purposes, since the allocation of costs is subjective and does not necessarily reflect the true response of costs to changes in production levels. Thus for decision-making purposes, variable costing (to be presented in the next chapter) is the preferred technique.

An income statement prepared using total accounting absorption costing provides a good measure of the firm's true profit for the period. This fact has been recognized by the accounting standard setting bodies, who require that full costing be used for external reporting purposes.

Chapter 3

Variable Costing

INFORMATION FOR DECISION MAKING

In addition to providing information for routine accounting statements used for control purposes (see Chapter 5 on budgetary control), accounting systems are an important source of information for decision-making purposes. Managers confront different kinds of decisions in the course of operations; some of these involve unique situations and require that management separate relevant from irrelevant factors in evaluating a set of alternatives. Examples of these special problems requiring decisions by management are:

1. What would be the effect on the firm's total profits of closing a department, or of opening a new department?

2. How will changes in the selling price and/or the sales volume of a particular product affect the firm's total income?

3. Should a particular component needed in the production process be purchased from an outside supplier or manufactured internally?

4. Should a special order from a potential customer be accepted or rejected?

The accounting information used in these situations should be clear, concise and **relevant** to the problem, to enable the best decisions to be reached by management. In particular, the information prepared by the accountant should incorporate only that data which is pertinent to the decision at hand. Accountants frequently speak of different costs for different purposes, a concept which is central to the use of variable costing for decision making in some situations. We will discuss the use of variable cost analysis in different circumstances, and demonstrate why it is appropriate in these contexts.

RELEVANT COSTS

The majority of decisions faced by management are, in essence, decisions involving a choice between alternative courses of action, strategies or policies. In making such decisions, considerable importance is attached to the identification of those costs that are relevant to the particular alternatives under consideration. The term relevant here means cost relating specifically to the choice to be made.

In evaluating the costs to be incurred in pursuing different strategies, care must be taken to identify the sunk costs, common costs and opportunity costs inherent in the alternatives. Costs incurred in the past, **sunk costs**, are not relevant in relation to a choice to be made concerning future actions. For example, in a situation where a particular manufacturing process already in use is to be evaluated against an alternative process requiring a large capital outlay, it is the **future** costs of the existing manufacturing process that should be compared against the future costs of the alternative. A common error is to perceive that an investment made in the past must be "recovered" before a change in policy can be profitable. (In fact, this error is common to many human decisions, from how long to wait for a bus to when to get out of Vietnam.) Maintenance costs, tax savings, and direct manufacturing costs are all relevant to the decision; the original investment in the existing process is not. Costs already incurred are only significant to the extent that they may predict future costs associated with a particular plan – for example, maintenance costs.

A second factor to be considered in any situation involving a choice between alternative strategies is that certain future costs may well arise under all of the alternatives. Because these costs are **common** to all alternatives and cannot be avoided, they should therefore have no influence upon which alternative is selected. In general terms, where a choice is to be made between alternative courses of action, only those costs that differ among the options should be considered; the other costs are irrelevant.

For example, suppose a firm has the option of converting a plant from its current use, the production of corrugated cardboard, to the manufacture of paperboard containers for packaged foods. In either case, the property taxes on the land and building will be the same, and need not be considered in comparing the two operating plans.

The above principle, which is sometimes called differential costing, also applies to a consideration of the revenues associated with alternative courses of action. Hence a comparison of outcomes of the alternatives to be decided upon can be made without the complicating effect of other factors that would remain unaffected, whichever alternative course of action is selected.

In decision making, the costs to be considered should also include relevant **opportunity costs**. The opportunity cost of an action is simply the net cash inflow which will be foregone due to a diversion of resources. For example, assume the cardboard manufacturer above will need access to a storage facility if it converts its plant to paperboard production. It already owns a warehouse, which it does not use currently and rents out for $25,000 a year. Since the firm owns the facility, it will not incur any cost in diverting the warehouse to its own use. However, it will lose $25,000 in rental receipts every year. This then is an opportunity cost of the conversion, and should be treated like any other cost when examining the alternatives.

THE CONCEPT OF VARIABLE COSTING

Many of the problems that confront management concern

short-term decisions; only rarely does it face long-term decisions such as whether or not to expand its capacity by the extension of an existing factory or merger with another business. Decisions relating to short-term considerations can normally be made on the assumption that the factory capacity and location will remain unchanged, whichever alternative is chosen. In fact many short-term courses of action have little or no effect on fixed overhead. Between alternative short-term strategies, the costs which differ are normally those which tend to vary in proportion to the levels of the various activities of the business, direct materials, direct labor and variable overhead. These costs are called variable costs.

As explained above, when choosing between alternative operating plans only those factors that are different need to be considered; common factors relating to all of the alternatives can be ignored. In view of the particular significance of variable costing when making a decision between alternative courses of action, the technique of variable costing (also referred to as direct costing or marginal costing) has been developed and is widely used as an aid to decision making.

Under variable costing, all costs are classified into the two categories of fixed and variable costs. Fixed costs are assumed to remain unchanged in the short term and are therefore common to all short-term decisions and may be ignored. Variable costing identifies changes in the variable costs as being the **relevant** costs when evaluating the results of short-term decisions.

Variable costing makes use of the concept of **contribution margin**, which is the difference between the variable costs of activities and the associated revenues. For a specific product, or group of products:

Sales revenue	*xx*
Less: variable costs of production	*yy*
Results in a contribution margin of	*zz*

The term contribution margin is not synonymous with net profit because only the variable costs of production are considered in its calculation. It has been shown in the preceding chapter that any allocation of fixed factory overhead to product cost is somewhat arbitrary, and the resulting product profit could be misleading. However, such problems rarely arise with the calculation of product contribution since sales revenue and variable costs are usually clearly identifiable with the relevant product or production flow. The contribution margins earned by specific products, or by groups of products, are added together to form a "pool" of total contribution for the business as a whole. Out of this "pool" are paid the fixed overhead expenses of the business. That part of the total contribution remaining is the profit of the business as a whole.

Where divisional profits can be attributed to specific products, the typical format for a variable costing statement is:

Product type	A	B	C	Total
Sales revenue	x	x	x	x
Variable costs	y	y	y	y
Contribution margin	z	z	z	z
Total fixed costs				w
Total profit				y

It should be noted that, under variable costing, no attempt is made to calculate a profit figure for individual products – it is the individual contributions that are calculated. The fixed costs are not allocated to, or absorbed by, the individual product types. Thus decisions based on variable costing statements will not be influenced by the accounting treatment of fixed overhead costs, as could happen under total absorption costing. Variable costing statements for internal reporting purposes have advantages and disadvantages associated with them. They provide useful information to management in the following ways:

1. By separating variable costs from the fixed cost component of production, a contribution margin statement calls attention to changes in the variable cost of production over time (for example, sharp increases in direct materials cost);

2. The contribution margin approach highlights the sensitivity of total profit to sales volume;

3. It directs management's attention to factors which are subject to manipulation in the short run.

Exclusive use of variable cost statements may not be desirable, however. Their two major disadvantages are:

1. They may cause management to be overly sensitive to short-term profitability, and hence likely to make decisions which compromise the future profits of the firm;

2. The clerical effort required to identify and record the variable component of costs may be extremely time consuming and the results unreliable.

PRACTICAL APPLICATIONS OF VARIABLE COSTING

Departmental performance analysis

The analysis of the relative performance of departments within a business is typically made by allocating total fixed overhead to the individual departments. The calculations of such allocations can be seen in the following example.

Department	A ($)	B ($)	C ($)	Total ($)
Sales revenues	20,000	50,000	25,000	95,000
Costs:				
Direct materials	1,000	15,000	10,000	26,000
Direct labor	3,000	16,000	14,000	33,000
Fixed overhead	2,000	7,000	9,000	18,000
Total costs	6,000	38,000	33,000	77,000
Profit for period	14,000	12,000	(8,000)	18,000

The statement shows a total profit of $18,000 for the period with departments A and B showing profits of $14,000 and $12,000 respectively, while department C shows a loss of $8,000. If these results were believed to be representative of the future performance of the departments management might consider closing down department C, with the intention of avoiding the $8,000 loss, and thus increasing profits to $26,000.

If, however, the results are restated using the variable costing format, the following statement is produced:

Department	A ($)	B ($)	C ($)	Total ($)
Sales	20,000	50,000	25,000	95,000
Variable costs	4,000	31,000	24,000	59,000
Contribution margin	16,000	19,000	1,000	36,000
Fixed overhead				18,000
Profit				$18,000

From this statement it can be seen that department C contributes $1,000 to the firm's profit and therefore should not be closed down. In fact, if it were closed down, its profit contribution would be lost and the firm's profit would be reduced to $17,000.

The reason for this apparent anomaly is that by closing department C management would not reduce fixed overhead by $9,000 as implied by the first accounting statement. The $9,000 charged to department C is merely an allocation of the total fixed overhead, none of which would actually be saved by closing the department. The $9,000 may be considered a common cost to the two alternatives, closing and maintaining Department C.

The presentation of accounting information using the variable costing format can help to focus management's attention on costs which would be affected by particular decisions.

Profit planning

It is frequently helpful to management to know how profits vary with sales volume. Using a contribution margin format this relationship may be observed directly. For example, assume that a business manufactures a single product which sells for $10 per unit with variable costs (direct materials, direct labor and variable overhead) of $5 per unit. Total fixed costs are $20,000 per month, at production volumes ranging from zero to ten thousand units.

Using this information the monthly profit that would be earned at various levels of activity can be calculated as follows:

Sales units	2,000	4,000	6,000	8,000	10,000
	($)	($)	($)	($)	($)
Sales revenue	20,000	40,000	60,000	80,000	100,000
Variable cost	10,000	20,000	30,000	40,000	50,000
Contribution	10,000	20,000	30,000	40,000	50,000
Fixed costs	20,000	20,000	20,000	20,000	20,000
Profit (loss)	(10,000)	0	10,000	20,000	30,000

Thus the firm's profits increase by $10,000 as production volume increases 20,000 units, or by $0.50 per unit. Obviously additional information would be necessary for management to determine how much to produce next year (most obviously, they need to estimate whether the market demand for 10,000 units exists).

This approach to profit planning is extended further in the next chapter, on break-even analysis. This analysis can easily be extended for a firm manufacturing more than one product type by calculating the contribution from each product type separately and adding these together to give the total contribution. Slight adaptations to the above format can also be made to assess the impact of changes in selling price.

Make or buy decisions

Consider a firm which manufactures a collapsible umbrella. A component wooden handle, used in its manufacture can be purchased from an outside supplier for $5, or can be manufactured internally by the firm. The decision whether to make or buy the component can be made by using variable costing. The firm's fixed costs will remain the same whichever course of action is taken, and therefore are irrelevant to the analysis. Assume also that there is spare productive capacity for the manufacture of the wooden handle and that the production costs per unit would be:

	($)
Direct materials	1.00
Direct labor	2.00
Variable overhead	1.00
Marginal cost of production	4.00

Hence, it would be cheaper to manufacture the component than to buy it from the outside supplier.

The situation is not as straightforward if full production capacity is being used to manufacture the umbrella. In this case some production of the umbrella would have to be curtailed to make available production capacity for the handle. Assume that the following details relate to the umbrella:

	($)	($)
Selling price per unit		16.00
Production costs per unit:		
Direct materials	6.00	
Direct labor	4.00	
Variable overhead	2.00	
Marginal cost of production		12.00
Contribution per unit		$4.00

The production rate per hour for the umbrella is 5 units and for the handle it is 10 units. Thus for each handle produced, the firm must forfeit the opportunity to produce one-half umbrella.

If some production capacity is switched from the umbrella to the handle, the contribution from the "lost" production of the umbrella will be forfeited. This is an opportunity cost of switching production from the umbrella to the handle. The effective cost of manufacturing a handle would thus become:

	($)
Marginal cost of production of the handle	4.00
Plus contribution of the umbrella forfeited during the time taken to produce the handle: 4.00×0.5	2.00
Effective cost per handle	6.00

Comparing the two alternatives, it may be observed that in these circumstances it would be cheaper to buy the component from the outside supplier.

Acceptance of an offer/special contracts

Sometimes management is presented with the opportunity to fill a special order (R) for a customer or to accept a particular contract on a one-time only basis. Variable costing is appropriate for decision making in these circumstances, since none of the firm's fixed costs would be affected by its decision. Example: Suppose that the product cost per unit of R is calculated as follows:

	($)
Direct materials	3.00
Direct labor	4.00
Overhead absorbed	4.00
Production cost	11.00
Selling price per unit	13.00

Assume that there is spare production capacity to produce up to 20,000 units of R above the current production level.

A potential customer offers to place an order for 15,000 units of R at a price of $9.00 per unit. It would appear that the offer does not even cover production costs and therefore should not be considered further. However, the overhead absorbed in the product cost of R includes both fixed and variable overhead. The variable would increase by only $1.00 per unit and there would be no effect on the fixed overhead of the business. As a common factor to each alternative, the fixed overhead is therefore not relevant to the decision to accept or reject the offer.

Using variable costing analysis, the marginal (i.e., variable) cost per unit of R is:

	($)
Direct material	3.00
Direct labor	4.00
Variable overhead	1.00
Production cost	8.00

Since the additional costs of producing each extra unit would be only $8.00, and the customer was prepared to pay $9.00 per unit, each extra unit would represent a profit contribution of $1.00. Hence the total contribution from the 15,000 unit special order (R) would increase the firm's profits by $15,000 (since the fixed cost remains unaltered, the total contribution of $15,000 would increase profits by the same amount). Marginal costing shows clearly that the order should be accepted.

This policy would apply to an additional order in a situation of surplus, in other words underutilized capacity. Care must be taken to ensure that these additional sales do not have any effect on existing sales, or if they do, that this effect is built into the calculations above. One would usually expect normal production volume to be sold at a price which would cover fixed overhead as well as marginal costs. There is a danger in committing for long periods spare productive capacity to special contracts which are priced on a marginal cost basis. Marginal costing will usually be appropriate only as a basis for pricing additional work to utilize surplus capacity when the duration of the additional work is relatively short, and other sales will not be affected. In the long run, prices must be set so that all costs of production are covered.

Allocation of scarce factors of production

In a firm manufacturing several products, a shortage of a common factor of production (e.g., a specialized category of skilled labor) might make it impossible for the firm to produce the desired quantities of all the products. The scarce factor of production is sometimes known as a limiting, critical, or constraining factor. In such a situation, management must decide upon the allocation of production which is the most efficient, or profitable, given the constraints imposed.

When a shortage of a common factor of production exists, total contribution margin will not necessarily be maximized by allocating production on the basis of the size of the contribution margin earned by each product. This is because a product which earns a relatively high contribution per unit might require a disproportionate amount of the scarce factor of production. Thus the scarce factor would be used up relatively quickly and no further production would be possible thereafter. The allocation problem is solved by determining which product earns the highest contribution per unit of scarce factor used. If production of the desired quantity of the product will leave some of the scarce factor of production unused, production is then allocated to the product which earns the next highest contribution per unit of scarce factor used, and the process of allocation is repeated until the supply of the scarce factor of production is exhausted.

Example: A business manufactures three products, X, Y, and Z, for which the following details apply:

	X	Y	Z
Desired production levels per month in units	1,000	2,000	500
Selling price per unit	$35.00	$25.00	$15.00
Variable cost per unit	15.00	10.00	5.00
Contribution margin per unit	20.00	15.00	10.00

A common factor of production, a rare plant oil, is in short supply, only 15,000 liters being available each month. Each unit of product X requires 20 liters of oil in its manufacture, each unit of product Y requires 5 liters of oil, and each unit of product Z requires 2 liters of oil. The contribution per liter of the scarce factor of production resulting from each product is calculated as follows:

	X	Y	Z
Contribution per unit	$20.00	$15.00	$10.00
Numbers of liters of oil required to manufacture one unit of product	20	5	2
Contribution earned by each product unit from one liter of scarce oil	$1.00	$3.00	$5.00

Thus, production will be allocated first to product Z, as this gives the highest contribution per liter of oil. The desired production level of Z, 500 units per month, will require 1,000 (500×2) liters of oil. Production will then be allocated to product Y, as this gives the next highest contribution per liter of oil. The desired production of Y, 2,000 units per month, will require 10,000 (2,000×5) liters of oil. Thus

11,000 liters per month of oil will be required by Z and Y, and this will leave only 4,000 liters of oil (i.e., $15,000 - 11,000$) available for the production of X. As each unit of X requires 20 liters of oil, the production of X will have to be limited to 200 units per month (i.e., $4,000 \div 20$).

By allocating production in this manner, total contribution is maximized. The calculations are left as an exercise for the student. Maximization of contributions ensures the maximization of profits. Any alternative allocation of production between X, Y and Z will reduce the total contribution. Linear programming is a rigorous mathematical method which can be used to allocate production in situations where there is a shortage of more than one common factor of production. This technique is described in some detail in any introductory textbook in operations research.

A COMPARISON OF VARIABLE COSTING AND TOTAL ABSORPTION COSTING

The above examples illustrate particular decisions which require the use of variable costing. Both variable costing and total absorption costing are useful costing techniques, provided they are used in the appropriate costing situation. Summarizing the last two chapters it may be said that:

1. Variable costing is easier to use, since the allocation of fixed overhead to individual products or departments is unnecessary.

2. The overhead allocation rates calculated under absorption costing reflect arbitrary assignments of overhead to departments. However, detailed knowledge of the functioning of an organization and the behavior of costs with respect to changes in activity volume can contribute to more reasonable overhead allocation.

3. Variable costing is preferable to full costing in most decision-making situations, particularly those of a short-term or special nature.

4. In the long run, overhead must be recovered if the business is to survive. Total absorption costing is an attempt to calculate a reasonable total production cost for a product, and may well form a better basis for long-term production and pricing decisions.

It should be noted again that variable costing is a method of analyzing costs for decision-making purposes. Under generally accepted accounting principles, for financial statements prepared for use by shareholders, variable costing is not an acceptable method for allocating costs since it will then understate product costs.

When preparing financial statements for external distribution, total absorption costing must be used; that is, all fixed

overhead must be included in the product cost. The resulting product will give shareholders a better idea of the total
cost of production, and thus provide a better estimate of the
firm's long run profitability.

Chapter 4

Profit Sensitivity Analysis

INTRODUCTION

One of the primary advantages of variable costing is that it facilitates the analysis of profit sensitivity to changes in sales or operating volume. Exclusive reliance on variable costing, however, is not appropriate in all decision contexts. For short run decisions, where the level of fixed costs will not change, variable costing provides management with the best analysis of the situation. However, in the long run, it is the primary concern of management to make a profit – that is, to see that all costs, both fixed and variable, are covered – and that an acceptable profit is earned for investors.

Before undertaking any new operating plan, management will want to evaluate its effect on overall profits, whether it is an increase in the sales price, a change in the sales mix, or a fixed sum allocated to advertising costs over a several-month period. Typically, management will want the answers to questions like one or more of the following:

1. What is the break-even point for this plan? That is, at what sales volume do we cover all of our costs, including both future and variable components?

2. At what sales volume will we realize a particular dollar profit?

3. If we have to reduce our selling prices due to pressure from competitors, but are able to maintain total sales volume, what will be the effect on profits?

4. If we grant an across-the-board cost-of-living raise, how much will sales volume have to increase to maintain last year's profit?

A single budget or forecasted income statement does not help management answer these questions, since it shows expected profit at one sales volume only. By using the information from a variable costing system and constructing a cost-volume-profit (C-V-P) chart, however, the accountant can highlight the sensitivity of profits to changes in activity volume, and thus help management to better understand the potential risks and rewards of a given operating plan.

In this chapter we will present the technique of cost-volume-profit analysis and demonstrate its usefulness in certain decision contexts. The student may note similarities between C-V-P analysis as presented here and variable costing as presented in the previous chapter. This is because the two approaches are not dissimilar, and in fact address the same basic question, "What is the effect of taking action x?" It may be convenient to think of variable costing as being a specific application of C-V-P, where the plan under consideration will not affect total fixed costs.

REVENUE AND COST BEHAVIOR

The construction of a cost-volume-profit chart requires as a first step a clear understanding of revenue and cost behavior over different activity volumes. For example, consider the short-term forecast operations of a single product manufacturing business that sells its products as they are made. Revenues and costs can be graphed as Figure 4 to show how they behave as output and sales vary.

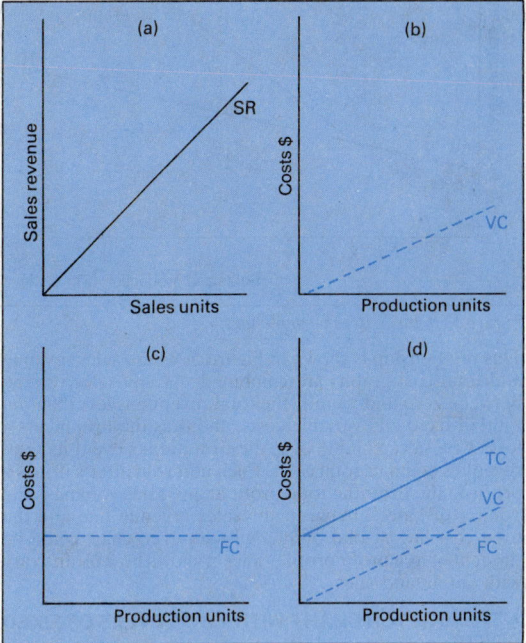

Figure 4. Cost behavior

1. Sales revenue: For a given selling price per unit, sales revenue (SR) will increase in direct proportion to the number of units sold. The sales revenue can be graphed as in section (a) of Figure 4.

2. Costs:

a. Variable costs, such as direct material, direct labor and variable overhead will be incurred in direct proportion to the level of production. Such costs can be graphed as in section (b) of Figure 4.

b. Fixed costs remain constant, over a limited range of production. As long as the proposal being evaluated is within that range, the costs may be graphed as in section (c) of Figure 4.

c. Total costs at any level of production are the sum of the fixed costs and the variable costs. They can be graphed as in section (d) of Figure 4.

A BASIC BREAK-EVEN CHART

Profit is the excess of sales revenue over total costs; when total costs exceed sales revenue a loss is incurred.

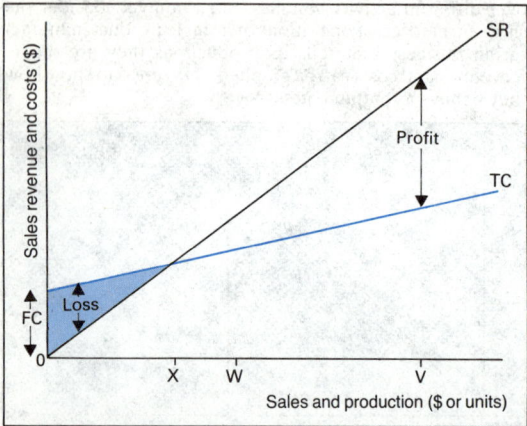

Figure 5. A basic break-even chart

This relationship is shown in Figure 5, where sales revenue and total cost graphs are combined. At any sales volume between zero and x units, the total revenue is less than the total of fixed and variable costs, and thus the firm incurs a loss. At a sales volume of x, the firm breaks even; its total revenues equal its total costs. Each unit sold after x brings a profit to the firm; the total profit at any sales volume is the "dollar distance" between the sales revenue line and the total cost line at that point. A break-even chart could be thought of as a profit profile, since it shows how profits vary with output and sales.

A BREAK-EVEN CHART WITH TWO LEVELS OF FIXED COSTS

What if management is considering a production plan that may require an additional fixed investment at some volume? Such a situation is presented in Figure 6. At sales volumes between zero and T, one factory is sufficient to meet the demand; at volumes greater than T, a new factory will have to be built. However, unless management anticipates sales volume greater than U, construction of a new plant would be decidedly unprofitable.

ADDITIONAL FORMATS AND INFORMATION

The contribution margin, introduced in the previous chapter, can be used as the basis for an alternative form of profit chart. Recall that if the selling price of a product exceeds its variable cost it may be said that such a product is (1) covering its variable cost, and (2) making a contribution towards the fixed overhead of the firm. Once volume is sufficient to have "covered" the total fixed costs of the firm, the contribution may be regarded as a contribution to the firm's total profit.

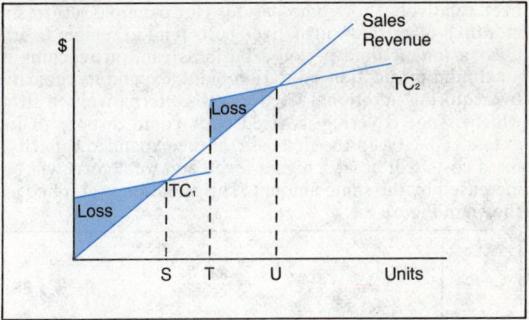

Figure.6. A break-even chart with two levels of fixed costs

The contribution margin concept can be seen in Figure 7. At sales level P it can be seen that the total contribution will not cover all the firm's fixed costs, so a loss is incurred. At sales level O the contribution more than covers the fixed costs, so a profit is realized. It should be noted that if a temporary reduction in sales to below the break-even point X occurs, it is still worth producing and selling the product since a contribution to fixed overhead is made. Halting production **altogether** would eliminate this contribution and result in a loss equal to the fixed costs, an amount which is greater than the loss suffered if any production and sales occur. This is the point which was made repeatedly in the discussion on variable costs; as long as the fixed costs are already committed, it is always better to produce and sell the product if sales revenue exceeds the total variable costs.

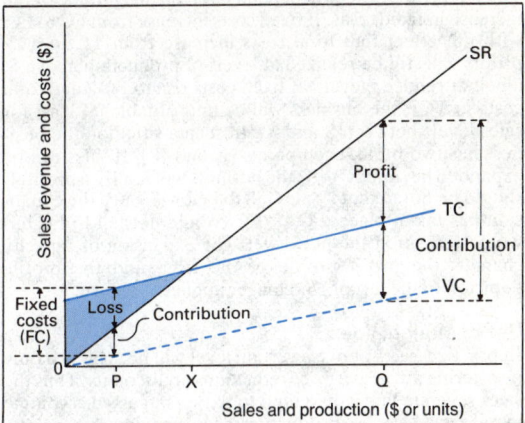

Figure 7. The concept of contribution

PROBLEMS AND LIMITATIONS OF BREAK-EVEN ANALYSIS
Time-scale and profit profiles
Profit profiles as shown are normally valid for a business

over relatively short time periods (for example, up to six months). Over that range, fixed costs tend to remain fixed. Over a longer time period a business can, on reaching a maximum production saturation point, expand its capacity by acquiring additional fixed assets. Alternatively, a firm which is not covering its fixed costs could dispose of its excess capacity. In the first case, at the expanded capacity, fixed costs will be at a higher level, and total costs will be increased by the same amount. This situation is graphed as shown in Figure 8.

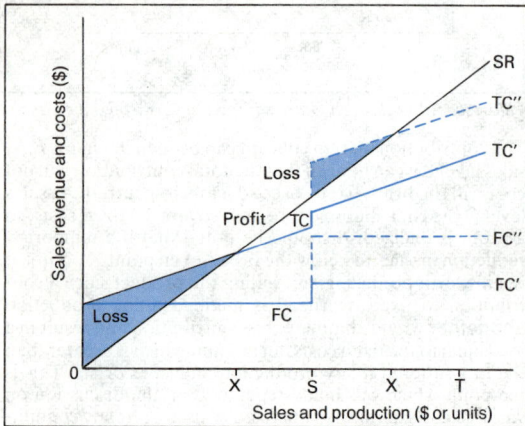

Figure 8. Expansion of capacity

The effect on profits will depend upon the magnitude of the increase in fixed costs. If fixed costs increase from FC to FC' with the effect that total costs increase from TC to TC', profits will still be realized at levels of production above S, albeit at reduced levels. If fixed costs rise to FC'', and total costs to TC'', the business will be unprofitable, at least for sales levels between S and X'. In such a situation the business has two break-even points (X and X'). If sales can be expanded beyond X' to T, the business will realize a profit. It should be noted that if sales fall to below S, once the expansion has taken place, FC' or FC'' would not fall to FC but would remain at the new level. The expansion of capacity changes the profit profile of the firm, and the profile depicted to the left of S no longer applies as shown.

Use of straight lines

In practice, sales above a certain level will be achieved only by offering attractive price reductions or discounts. Thus the sales revenue line would tend to flatten out as sales volume increases. Also, as production nears maximum capacity, additional production overtime is required, machine breakdowns increase, and general efficiency usually diminishes. Thus the total cost line tends to rise fairly sharply as output nears maximum capacity. These two phenomena combined may have a significant effect on profits, and make reliance on break-even charts unreliable under such circumstances. Subject to this limitation, it is quite common to find that straight-line assumptions still result in acceptable approximations for organizations working at normal levels of production.

CALCULATION METHODS FOR BREAK-EVEN ANALYSIS

As an alternative to graphical representation, algebraic calculations of break-even points can be made. Manipulation of the basic relationships between sales volume, costs and profits

Revenues=fixed costs+variable costs+profits

will yield some insights into profit sensitivity to changes in activity level. In the following simplified examples we will illustrate various uses of the algebraic approach. A set of questions and answers using the break-even formula will be presented.

A single-product firm

Assume an organization is able to sell a particular product for $5 per unit. Variable costs of production are $3 per unit. Fixed costs total $10,000. Current sales are 6,000 units.

1. What is the current level of profits?

At a sales level of 6,000 units, total revenue is $30,000. Total variable costs are $18,000, and fixed costs are $10,000. Profit is therefore $2,000.

2. What is the break-even volume for the organization?

The break-even point is where profit is zero, or Total Revenue=Total Costs. Since the selling price is $5 per unit, Revenue=5x, where x is the number of units sold. Total variable costs are 3x, and total fixed costs are $10,000, regardless of the production volume. The break-even point therefore occurs where $5x=10,000+3x$, at a sales volume of 5,000 units.

3. What is the current safety margin?

The safety margin is the amount by which current sales exceed break-even sales. With current sales of 6,000 units, the safety margin is 1,000 units, or about 17%.

4. What sales volume is necessary to make a profit of $5,000, given the same revenue and cost structure?

$$\text{Revenues} - \text{fixed costs} - \text{variable costs} = \text{profit}.$$
$$5x \quad - \quad 10,000 \quad - \quad 3x \quad = 5,000$$

If an advertising campaign costing $2,000 was undertaken, management estimates that

1. 2,000 more units could be sold at $5 per unit, or
2. Price could be increased to $5.50 with sales volume remaining at 6,000 units.

Which strategy should be adopted?

If the advertising campaign is undertaken, fixed costs will increase to $12,000. Hence profits under the first option are:

$(8,000 \times \$2) - \$12,000 = \$4,000$

and under the second option are:

$(6,000 \times \$2.50) - \$12,000 = \$3,000$

Comparing the two options with the current level of profits, the first alternative, undertaking the advertising campaign but leaving the price of the product at $5, is preferred.

A multi-product firm

Most firms, and even most internal divisions of a single firm, do not sell a single product, but rather a number of products which have different unit prices and production costs. In this section we show how to adapt the break-even analysis to such cases. Assume a university-sponsored day-care center accepts both the children of faculty members, for which it is reimbursed by the university, and the children of families in the community, who pay for the service privately. The day-care center has the following mix of clients and cost and revenue structure:

Type of Child		Charges
Faculty	80%	$900 per year
Community	20%	$1,200 per year

The fixed costs are $13,400 per year; in addition, it costs $2.50 per child per day for meals and supervision. Assume the day-care center is in operation 250 days per year.

What is the break-even point for the center? Since private clients and university clients pay different fees for the day care, in order to calculate the break-even point it is necessary to assume some mix of children. The university has a policy of accepting one child from the community for every four children from the faculty. We can use, therefore, an average revenue figure of $1,000 ($0.80 \times \$900 + 0.20 \times \$1,200$) per child. The problem is then solved using the standard break-even formula:

$$\$1,000x = \$13,400 + (250 \times \$2.50)x$$

Assuming the day-care center maintains its current faculty/community child ratio of 4 to 1, they will break even with an enrollment of 36 children. (Obviously if the calculation results in a non-integer solution, the break-even point would have to be reduced to the first feasible solution. It would not be possible, for example, to serve twelve and a half neighborhood children.)

Suppose the federal government sponsors a program which

will subsidize the meals of the community children, reducing the variable cost per day to $2.20 per child for each non-faculty family. The day-care administrators estimate that the clerical cost of participating in the program will increase their fixed costs by $250 per year. If they wish to maintain the current ratio of 4 faculty children to 1 community child, What is the new break-even point under the government subsidy program?

To calculate the new break-even point, we need to find the average variable cost per child, the same way we found the average revenue per child. At the 4 to 1 mix, this cost will be $2.44 [($2.50×0.8)+($2.20×0.2)]. The new fixed cost will be $13,650. Therefore we can find the new break-even point as:

$$1,000x = \$13,650 + (250 \times \$2.44x)$$

The new break-even point is at an enrollment of 35 children.

What if the day-care center decides that the government subsidy should be passed along directly to the families of the community in the form of reduced fees? They want to retain the current ratio of 4 to 1, and still break even at an enrollment of 40 children. How much can they lower the fee charged the community families under these conditions?

In this case we are not solving for the break-even point, which we have determined, but for the total revenues which will allow us to realize this break-even point. The same formula can be used, but we now solve for a different variable:

$$(0.8 \times 40 \times \$900) + (0.2 \times 40 \times \text{New Fee})$$
$$= \$13,650 + (\$2.44 \times 40 \times 250)$$

The new fee is then about $1.156. We could have arrived at the same answer by dividing the total savings—($0.30×250×8)−$250—by the total number of children from the community and subtracting that amount from the original fee.

SUMMARY

Profit sensitivity analysis can provide management with a first approximation of the risks to be undertaken in any new project. The break even format can be used to analyze the effects of changes in sales prices, manufacturing costs or other elements of management's operating plans.

Chapter 5

Planning and Budgeting

PLANNING FOR OBJECTIVES AND CONTROL

The need for forward planning

Most major businesses prepare long-term plans, expressed in financial terms, for periods of at least five years ahead. The plans show, in general terms, the expected scale and results of operations in each of those years, and the expected financial outcomes.

The business environment is constantly changing, reflecting such things as technological development, variations in demand, changes in consumer tastes and the overall economy. A business can rarely remain successful by providing the same product to the same market indefinitely. The most successful businesses tend to look ahead for several years, identify significant changes that may occur, and plan appropriate action well in advance. Particular factors which require careful consideration and planning include:

1. Developments in technology, which tend to reduce the product life-cycle, and render existing methods of production obsolete.

2. Increased competition in a particular market or the development of substitute products by other firms.

3. Capital requirements to increase or replace production facilities, and the associated sources of finance.

The increasing complexity of business requires clear objectives on such things as profits, return on investment and market share. In large organizations, such objectives can only be achieved by coordinated long-term planning throughout the organization.

Long-term plans of this type are usually prepared on a "rolling" basis, which means that every year the current year's figures drop out and another year is added to the end of the plan. Such plans indicate the actions necessary to achieve the desired long-term corporate objectives.

Budgeting as planning

Budgeting is the process of preparing a detailed operating plan for a specific period of time, usually the next fiscal year. Some firms budget for longer or shorter periods than a single year, but the process is of a different nature and serves a different purpose than that of long-term planning. Among these differences are the following:

1. Plans for the next year can be made in considerably more detail than those for later years. The budgeting process forces management to anticipate some of the problems or opportunities which will confront them during the year.

2. Plans for the next year can be far more accurate, since the effects of general economic conditions, and specific changes in product markets can be estimated with more precision over a relatively short time horizon.

3. The long-term corporate plan assists the attainment of corporate objectives, but the budget plays a more important role in motivating managers. Participation in the budgeting process can help to outline each manager's area of responsibility, and can foster goal congruence between individual managers and the corporation.

4. The budget can be a useful tool for management control. By establishing performance goals, the budget provides a standard against which actual results may be compared at the end of the period. The process of reviewing operating results in this way serves to focus managers' attention on those areas where problems may exist.

THE BUDGETING PROCESS
Nature of the budget
A budget can represent a formalization of management's expectations, it may serve as an instrument of coordination for the plans of all of a firm's divisions, it can be a source of motivation or an instrument of control. A budget represents the policy of the firm that is to be pursued by all staff during the following year. It is, in effect, an instruction from the chief executive and directors, setting out what the staff are to achieve in the following year. Sales staff are committed to attain the level of sales formulated in the budget, and those responsible for managing departments or cost centers within the business are instructed not to incur costs in excess of the levels shown in the budget. It is a significant feature of the budget that, for each individual part of the budget, a manager is made responsible for its fulfillment. In practice some degree of devolution of responsibility may take place, but someone, perhaps at more than one managerial level, will be specifically responsible for the attainment of each part of the budget.

Top management's objectives
Some time before the beginning of a financial year, forecasts of economic activity are reviewed by top management along with the results of the previous year's operations. Sometimes these figures are accompanied by analyses of particular industries or markets whose activities would affect the firm's performance. With this input, management sets overall objectives for the firm, usually expressed in terms of the previous year's and/or net income figures. For example, the president might state that he would like to see a 10% increase in sales and a 15% increase in net income, implying that he would also like to see marketing and manufacturing costs decrease as sales increased.

Preparation of the budget
Top management's objectives are communicated to the

individual division managers, who are then asked to prepare forecasts of their activities to meet the objectives. The individual forecast will be expressed in financial as well as physical terms, and will be closely scrutinized by top management (or the budget committee where applicable). Top management should ensure that the individual forecasts for all aspects of the business are compatible with each other. For example, the planned level of production, when coupled with existing inventory levels, must provide enough units to match the planned level of sales; planned levels of manpower and machine capacity must be sufficient to manufacture the required production. A uniformity of approach and presentation is important in this process as is the need for full consultation between top management and individual managers. Larger companies formalize the procedure by setting up a budget committee and by using a procedural budget manual. The detailed preparation work should be coordinated by a senior accounting official, usually the management accountant.

Operating plans and budgets must be prepared and coordinated for all of the activities of the firm. The marketing and production departments will prepare separate budgets for their departments, and will outline their requirements in order to meet the firm's objectives. Production schedules and required inventory levels will be specified in these operating plans. A cash budget and a capital budget will need to be prepared for the firm as a whole so that appropriate plans may be made to supply each division with the resources needed to meet its objectives.

The profit plan
When acceptable and compatible plans and budgets have been determined for each aspect of the business, they are drawn together by top management to form a profit plan for the forthcoming year. This forecast is reviewed in light of organizational objectives and a decision is reached as to whether it represents an acceptable plan for the next year, given the economic conditions expected to prevail. Forecasts are frequently revised if the projected profit is insufficient. The master forecast is then formally approved by top management, at which stage it becomes the budget. Each division is then committed to meeting the target figures in the profit plan. If the budgeting process has encouraged participation at all levels, the profit plan should represent attainable performance standards to all divisions committed to it.

The capital budget
Preparation of the profit plan requires management to assess its needs for additional plant and equipment to meet its objectives. Detailed proposals for the financing of capital projects are referred to as capital budgets. The evaluation of alternative sources of financing (short-term debt, long-term debt, sale of common stock, restriction of dividend payments) is at the heart of the capital budgeting process, and is

usually not the responsibility of the managerial accountant. Sometimes a firm will have more proposals for capital projects than it can undertake at one time, necessitating some ranking of the projects in line with the firm's overall priorities. Comparative analysis of the profitability of competing capital projects is the subject of Chapter 8.

Cash budgeting

In a firm, the individual budgets for sales, materials, labor and overhead costs will each have a corresponding cash implication. The resulting estimated cash receipts and cash disbursements are recorded in the cash budget. As with the other budgets, this is usually prepared on a monthly basis and shows the estimated bank balance at the end of the month. It is frequently the case that cash resources are a limiting factor with regard to an organization's goals. It is important therefore to plan cash resources carefully, to prevent unanticipated cash shortages, and to avoid holding large amounts of cash idle for any length of time. Where cash shortfalls are expected, arrangements for short-term bank loans can usually be made in advance. Many firms maintain a **line of credit** with a bank, which guarantees them, for a small service charge, a certain amount of borrowing privileges on very short notice. Where short-term borrowing is infeasible or expensive for a firm, operating plans need to be changed to eliminate cash shortfalls. Detailed cash budgeting is an essential ingredient in any budgetary system. As with all budgets, once agreed upon by top management, it acts as an authorization to the financial manager to proceed with cash management as specified. In turn he is responsible for monitoring cash resources and advising management of any divergences from budget.

PREPARATION OF THE CASH BUDGET

The preparation of a cash budget is best illustrated by the use of a simplified example of a new firm commencing at the beginning of January next year. Budgeted profits for the first three months are as follows:

Month	January ($)	February ($)	March ($)
Sales	100,000	120,000	160,000
Expenses:			
Materials	30,000	36,000	48,000
Wages	10,000	16,000	18,000
Overhead	50,000	50,000	50,000
Depreciation	2,500	2,500	2,500
Profit	7,500	15,500	41,500

It is estimated that $75,000 in capital will be contributed to the firm at its inception, and that $60,000 will be spent on equipment in January, and $57,000 in February. Twenty per cent of sales are expected to be in cash, and eighty per cent on credit. The experience of other firms with customers in the same area leads management to expect collection of the accounts receivable, on average, one month later. Materials are paid for in the month in which they are purchased. Seventy-five per cent of wages are paid at the end of the month in which the services are rendered, and the remaining twenty-five per cent is paid in the next month. Overhead expenses are paid one month after the month in which they were incurred.

No raw materials inventory is held in January and February, as materials are purchased as required. In March, purchases total $49,000, with $1,000 of this held in inventory at the end of the month. There is no work in process at the end of any of the first three months.

The cash budget for the first three months is shown below.

Month	January ($)	February ($)	March ($)
Beginning balance	0	(2,500)	(11,000)
Cash inflows:			
Paid in capital	75,000	0	0
Cash sales	20,000	24,000	32,000
Collections from customers	0	80,000	96,000
Total inflows:	95,000	104,000	128,000
Cash outflows:			
Equipment	(60,000)	(57,000)	0
Materials	(30,000)	(36,000)	(49,000)
Wages:			
Current	(7,500)	(12,000)	(13,500)
Accrued	0	(2,500)	(4,000)
Overhead	0	(5,000)	(5,000)
Total outflows:	(97,500)	(112,500)	(71,500)
Ending balance	(2,500)	(11,000)	45,500

The depreciation charge is an accounting adjustment to expense the cost of capital equipment purchases over a number of accounting periods. This has no effect on cash and the depreciation charge is excluded from the cash budget.

The cash budget shows that a negative bank balance is to be expected during the first month of operations, with an $11,500 cash deficit expected at the end of February. In March receipts will exceed disbursements by $56,500, so the bank balance is expected to be $45,000 by the end of that month. Prior to the beginning of operations, the firm would need to arrange with a bank for a line of credit to cover the expected cash shortfall in January.

The reliability of the cash budget depends on the accuracy of management's forecasts of sales, collectibility of accounts receivable, and the amount and timing of cash outflows necessary to maintain normal business operations. Failure to prepare a cash budget, or careless estimation of the factors affecting cash receipts and disbursements, could result in unnecessary and potentially serious cash problems. Even an apparently profitable enterprise, as the one in the example above, could suffer serious cash shortages at times during its operations.

BUDGETING AS AN ITERATIVE PROCESS

Budgeting is an activity which is best accomplished on an iterative basis: that is, objectives, plans and proposals should move back and forth between levels of management until a consensus is reached. The budgeting process is not simply a means of getting numbers onto a formal document. It is a communication process, and as such can be very valuable to a firm. Ideally, information will be exchanged in the course of preparing the budget, rather than being a process of argument and rebuttal.

ASPECTS OF BUDGETARY CONTROL

Performance Appraisal

Accounting statements, such as an income statement, show results achieved but are not necessarily an appropriate measure of organizational performance. For example, in times of severe recession, a modest loss for a period, as measured on the income statement, might be a creditable achievement in the prevailing adverse circumstances. In order to appraise performance, the actual results achieved should be compared against a suitable benchmark. A meaningful and informative method of performance appraisal is to compare actual results and data against the budgeted results. Budgets can be prepared in great detail for all parts of an organization, and the actual results, presented in the same degree of detail, can be compared against them. This comparison will reveal whether costs and revenues, of specific departments or cost centers, are in excess of, or below, the levels that had been forecast by management and incorporated in the budgets. Remedial action can be taken where appropriate. This process is referred to as budgetary control.

Periodic comparison

Given that budgetary control is concerned with identifying areas in which remedial action is necessary, it is clear that budgets need to be sub-divided into shorter periods for control purposes. Control reports must be prepared early enough to influence actual results and reduce further divergences from the budget. Monthly reports are common. Reports should be prepared as soon as possible after the end of the control period.

Review of variances

The amounts by which actual results diverge from budgeted results are called variances. The profit (or loss) variance is the difference between actual costs (and revenues) and the corresponding budgeted costs and revenues. When actual costs have exceeded budgeted costs, the situation is undesirable and the variance is called an unfavorable variance. Conversely, when actual costs are less than budgeted costs, the situation is desirable and the variance is called a favorable variance. Variance analysis highlights the areas where greater control would appear to be necessary.

Variance analysis

Actual results may differ from budgeted results for myriad reasons, and thus the simple comparison of the two may not provide management with sufficient information to take corrective action. For example, actual sales revenue for a period might be less than budgeted revenue for any or all of the following reasons:

1. Sales volume in units was below the budgeted level;

2. Due to deliberate or inadvertent (i.e., offering a volume discount which most customers took advantage of) action on management's part, average selling price was below the budgeted selling price;

3. The sales mix differed from the planned mix; for example, sales were projected at a 65/35 ratio for two products, but actual sales were at a 55/45 mix.

Each of these sources of variance could lead management to a different interpretation of the underlying cause, and suggest different strategies for subsequent periods. A similar observation may be made regarding all the line item variances on an income statement. In Chapters 6 and 7 we will investigate in detail the preparation and interpretation of variance analyses from budgeted and actual results.

The influence of budgets on behavior

Accounting systems do not always have a passive or neutral effect on those who participate in them and this is particularly so in relation to budgeting systems. Since the relationship of a manager's performance to the budget is usually an important part of his overall performance appraisal, managers often regard it with some distaste or even hostility. It has been argued that the methods of preparation and operation of budgets and budgetary control systems can have a very significant effect on the attitudes and hence behavior of managers who have a responsibility for the fulfillment of sections of the overall budget. Recall that the budget is often used by top management to satisfy two purposes: to motivate managers to achieve the corporate objectives embodied in the budget, and to provide a benchmark against which managers' performance can be evaluated.

Participative and authoritarian budgets

With regard to the first of the two roles outlined above, many people (both managers and behavioral researchers) believe that maximum motivation is achieved in situations where managers can identify themselves with the budgetary process. This may be interpreted to mean that managers are most committed to attaining the budget's goals when they have played a leading part in the formulation of the budget, and where any amendments made by top management to the managers' forecasts at the time of the budget preparation have been fully discussed with the managers concerned and their agreement to the amendments has been obtained. Where managers have been fully involved, the budgetary process is said to be participative by nature, and a sense of harmony and motivation may be achieved. By contrast, when top management imposes budgets on managers with little or no consultation or agreement, a feeling of hostility and alienation may arise among managers. Here the budgetary process is said to be authoritarian in nature. Managers frequently feel no personal identification with the budget and will often consider, in these circumstances, that all or parts of the budget are unreasonable or undesirable. If this is so they will probably not pursue the budget policy with the maximum possible commitment.

Budgets as targets

Sometimes top management establishes performance standards that are so unrealistic that it is clearly not possible to meet them. Top management may consider that unattainable standards present a constant challenge and incentive to managers. On the other hand, if the budget is set too high, managers may perceive the impossible nature of the target and cease to treat the budget seriously. An added disadvantage is that a high budget almost inevitably leads to high adverse variances being reported, with an implicit criticism of a manager's ability. A manager who has performed exceptionally well, and has come close to achieving an impossibly high budget, is not likely to react favorably to such criticism. Unrealistically high budgets will probably be ignored by managers and variance analysis will provide little insight into performance evaluation. There is evidence to suggest that maximum motivation is likely to occur with tight budgets which are perceived to be attainable. Experiments with implicit budgets have also produced some interesting results, which tend to suggest that giving greater freedom to managers to set their own goals may in fact result in better performance. Most studies on budgets and motivation indicate quite clearly that low budgets are usually associated with low performance.

Goal congruence

Managerial behavior may also be influenced by the rewards that are perceived to be available for regular achievement of budget results. If such desirable outcomes for the managers as enhanced salary awards or increased promotional prospects are seen to exist, both the personal goals of the managers and the goals and objectives of the organization will be realized by the attainment of the budget. Thus the actions of the managers will be in harmony with the objectives of the organization. This situation is described as goal congruence. The budgetary control system should be designed so that, as far as is possible, the goals of the individual managers are

consistent with the goals of the organization as a whole.
Incentive systems based on short-term results, combined
with emphasis on long-term planning, will lead to incompatible goals for the individual and the firm, and incompatible
goals result in dissonance. Individual managers, seeking
salary and promotional rewards, might favor courses of
action which show short-term favorable results, even if the
longer-term implications for the organization are less favorable. Or if generous cost budgets are set, based largely on
the level of the previous year's actual expenditures, and no
significant rewards are perceived by managers for achieving
savings, managers may deliberately spend up to their
budgeted allowance simply to prevent tighter budgets being
imposed in the future.

Discretionary costs
In order to be effective for control and performance evaluation purposes, the working of the system must be seen to be
fair and unbiased to the participant managers. Managers
should only be held responsible for those costs that they
actually control. This is particularly important in the allocation of overhead costs to individual departments. Certain
allocation schemes, while perfectly acceptable for product
costing purposes, may impose a "tax" on particular divisions which is beyond the control of the manager. Thus
attention should be paid to the controllability of the costs for
which managers are being held responsible.

Advantages of budgetary control
The advantages to an organization of a system of budgetary
control can be summarized briefly as follows:

All parts of the organization are critically appraised from
the point of view of profitability and cost. The operating and
financial budgets of the organization permit anticipation of
the firm's requirements for the forthcoming year. Working
capital requirements are planned in advance. The objectives
of the organization are communicated to staff in operational
terms and diverse activities are thereby coordinated.
Responsibility can be decentralized and motivating targets
can be established for managers. Control and performance
evaluation are established by means of a periodic review of
variances.

Chapter 6

Standard Costs for Direct Material and Direct Labor

RATIONALE FOR STANDARD COSTS

Standard costs are central to the process of management control in most manufacturing firms, as well as many service organizations. A standard cost represents a performance objective, that is a quantitative expression of the amount of resources that are expected to be consumed in order to produce a specific output. When budgets are prepared, they are expressed (explicitly or implicitly) in terms of standard costs. By comparing actual operating costs to standard operating costs for a period, management can identify those areas of its operation which require possible corrective action.

In the previous chapter, the technique of variance analysis was introduced as a method by which management could find potential problem areas by comparing budgeted costs to actual costs for a period. This practice is often referred to as **management by exception**, indicating that managers devote their time only to those activities where the actual performance departs significantly from the standard. In this chapter we will demonstrate how the use of standard costs will help management to identify specific causes of favorable and unfavorable variances.

DERIVATION OF STANDARD COSTS

Standard costs are derived from long-run average performance under normal conditions, and as such do not represent ideal performance objectives, but currently attainable ones. Frequently historical performance data is supplemented by engineering estimates of the quantity and the cost of materials and labor input necessary to achieve a given amount of output under efficient operating conditions. However, theoretical estimates of standard production costs should never be substituted for estimates based on actual performance data, since a standard is intended to allow for a "normal" amount of spoilage or lost labor time due to machine breakdowns. The standard cost of a product will include the standard material cost, standard labor cost, and standard overhead cost.

STANDARD COSTS FOR DIRECT MATERIALS AND DIRECT LABOR

Standard materials price

The standard materials price represents the best estimate by management of the average price the purchasing department must pay per unit of material for the coming year. The standard materials price should take into account the quality or grade of material required in the manufacturing pro-

cess, and should be adjusted for expected discounts and
normal handling charges.

Standard materials quantity

The standard materials quantity represents in physical units
the amount of material expected to be used in producing
one unit of output. The amount of input allowed per unit of
output will usually exceed the amount of materials contained in the finished product. This is because a certain
amount of material will inevitably end up on the factory
floor as waste, or be mislaid in the manufacturing process.
Thus the specifications for a cotton shirt produced in mass
quantities might call for one yard of material per shirt.
However, the standard materials quantity might be 1.02
yards per shirt, allowing for 2% spoilage on the average.

Standard labor rate

The standard labor rate, or wage rate, is the labor equivalent
of the standard material price. It represents management's
best estimate of the average cost per hour of the labor
required in the production process. Overtime will be
excluded from this estimate unless the firm relies upon a
certain amount of overtime to meet production quotas
under normal circumstances.

Standard labor quantity

The standard labor quantity represents the estimated
number of hours (or fraction of an hour) required to produce one unit of output under normal conditions. As with
the standard materials quantity, the standard may be
slightly more than the actual production time to allow for a
normal amount of down time or labor "inefficiency."

USES OF STANDARD COSTS

Although the focus in this chapter is on the use of standard
costs in the preparation of variance reports for control purposes, they are used within an organization for other
reasons as well. Chief among these is the fact that standard
costs facilitate record-keeping; if products were kept on the
corporation's books at actual costs, it would be tedious to
maintain accurate records of the direct costs of the products
as they are transferred from raw materials inventory to work
in process to finished goods inventory. Maintaining a record
of the actual indirect cost of each unit would be impossible,
since the overhead attributable to each product unit
depends upon the total number of units produced. The use
of standard costs also reduces managerial time required to
prepare budgets, assemble the data for and interpret special
cost studies, and provide cost estimates of particular jobs or
products.

CALCULATING STANDARD MATERIALS AND
LABOR VARIANCES

To illustrate the calculation of material and labor variances,
consider the data in Figure 9 for the Tyrone Company,
which makes a single product. The actual operating results

for the month of August are compared to the budgeted results for the same month.

The direct costs for the period show a small unfavorable variance of $1,300. If management simply concentrated on total sales dollars and total costs, they might mistakenly attribute the large variance to the lower than budgeted sales volume in units. However, closer examination of the operating results shows that the actual direct cost per unit of output was $1.50 more than the standard cost. This number is found by dividing the total budgeted costs by the budgeted units, and comparing that unit cost, $18.50, to the unit cost derived from total actual costs divided by total actual units, $20.00.

	Budgeted costs	Actual costs	Variance
Units	7,000	6,540	
Variable costs:			
Direct material	87,500	82,500	5,000 F
Direct labor	42,000	48,300	6,300 U
Total costs	129,500	130,800	1,300 U
Unit cost	18.50	20.00	1.50 U

F = favorable   U = unfavorable

Figure 9. Tyrone Company

Even this figure does not provide much information to management, since the source of the increased manufacturing costs is still not obvious. Management needs to know the source of the increased manufacturing costs so that they can investigate the underlying causes where necessary. Was the raw materials cost higher than expected, or was there more spoilage than anticipated? Did the expected wage rate increase, or was labor working less efficiently than the standard required?

To find the answers to these questions, management needs a breakdown of the standard costs of a product unit. Ignoring overhead costs for now, the direct material and direct labor standard costs are:

	$
Direct Materials:	
2.5 pounds @ $5.00 per pound	12.50
Direct Labor:	
0.5 labor hours @ $12.00 an hour	6.00
Standard Unit cost	18.50

Using the format outlined in Figure 10, these standard costs can be used to calculate very specific information about the sources of the total direct manufacturing cost variance. Inserting the data from our firm's August production figures, we find the following variances. We will assume that the amount of raw materials purchased was equal to the amount used during the month, so that there was no increase in raw materials inventory.

Direct Materials:

15,000 lb.	15,000 lb.	16,350 lb.
$5.50 per lb.	$5.00 per lb.	$5.00 per lb.
$82,500	$75,000	$81,750

$7,500 U $6,750 F

The first calculation gives us $82,500, the actual cost for the actual amount of material used during the period. The second calculation gives us $75,000, the standard materials cost of the actual quantity of material used during the period (as if the material had been purchased at the standard price). The difference between these two, $7,500, represents the part of the variance attributable to the difference in prices, or the **materials price variance**. The third calculation gives us $81,750, the standard materials cost for the output produced, had the standard amount of material been used and purchased at the standard price. The difference between the latter two figures represents the amount of the total materials variance which can be attributed to materials usage, or the **materials quantity variance**.

The same process is followed to find the direct labor variances. The method is outlined in Figure 11 below.

Direct Labor:

4,200 hrs.	4,200 hrs.	3,270 hrs.
$11.50 per hr.	$12.00 per hr.	$12.00 per hr.
$48,300	$50,400	$39,240

$2,100 F $11,160 U

Just as in the materials variances, the difference in the first two calculations gives us the **labor rate variance**, or the amount of the total variance we may attribute to an unexpected change in wage rates. In this case, note that the variance is favorable, indicating that we actually paid less per hour of labor time than we budgeted. However, this fact makes all the more troublesome the labor usage variance, since it must be very large to result in a total unfavorable labor variance of $9,060. Indeed, the labor usage variance is quite large, $11,160.

Note that the total materials variance, $750 unfavorable, and the total labor variance, $9,060 unfavorable, are not the same as those reported in Figure 9 (Tyrone Company). This

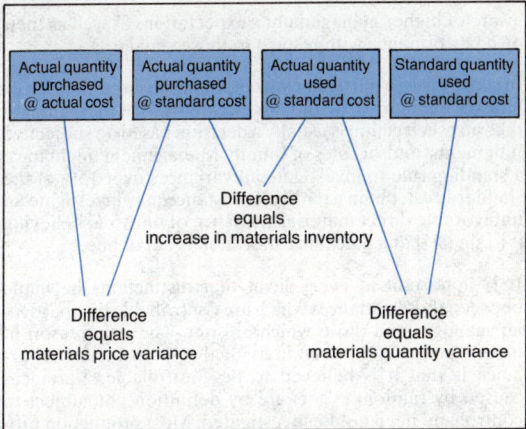

Figure 10. Calculations for direct materials variances

is because, for the purpose of controlling direct manufacturing costs, management is not concerned with the lower production volume. Of course, the reduction in the volume is not irrelevant to management, but its effect will be examined in a different context, when management undertakes **profit analysis**. This process is discussed in some detail in Chapter 9.

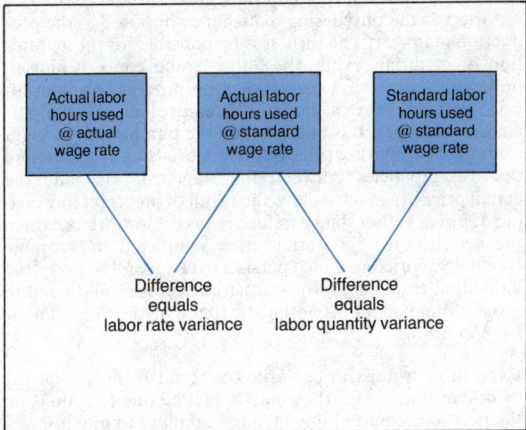

Figure 11. Calculations for direct labor variances

REPORTING THE VARIANCES

Once management has calculated the direct materials and direct labor variables, it must decide what action, if any, to take to correct the variances. In most firms, the variances are reported to the individual departments as a routine matter, whether or not management believes they warrant further inquiry. This feedback helps keep subordinates aware of higher management's expectations as well as their own performance with respect to those standards.

In some cases, a particular variance may be large enough, or unusual enough, to warrant investigation. Whether or not to take any such action is usually a decision based on subjective judgments, and/or rules of thumb. Management might have a standing rule to investigate all variances over 15% of the standard cost, but in a particular instance may investigate an unfavorable direct materials variance of only 5%, believing it to signal that a machine calibration is out of line.

It is important at every level that distinctions be made between those variances which are controllable by a particular manager and those which are not. The only reason to investigate, or to hold an individual responsible for, a variance is that it is believed to be controllable. Variances caused by random events are by definition not subject to control and need not be investigated. Most production processes will show variances on a regular basis, and within some range these will be considered normal. Those variances selected for further investigation should include those for which the expected benefit from the investigation exceeds the expected cost.

CONTROLLABILITY AND VARIANCE REPORTING

Materials price variance

In most companies, the materials price variance would be reported to the purchasing manager as opposed to the production manager. The former is responsible for the acquisition of materials, while the latter would concern himself only with their use in the production process. A materials price variance may or may not be controllable by the purchasing manager. It is unlikely that the purchasing manager can affect the market price of the materials he acquires, and thus discrepancies between the standard price and the actual price are in most cases the result of incorrect forecasting of prices rather than a failure to take appropriate care in the acquisition of materials. If a significant unfavorable (favorable) price variance persists over several periods, the individual responsible for price forecasting would need to be cautioned about his optimistic (pessimistic) view of market conditions.

Even though most price variances result from forecasting errors, in some cases they may in fact be due to actions on the part of the purchasing manager. Failure to monitor raw materials inventory levels closely might force the manager to buy on the spot market or at inflated prices in order to avoid a shortage. Alternatively, the purchasing manager may elect to purchase higher- or lower-quality material than that specified in the product standards. The wisdom of such a substitution should be jointly determined by the purchasing and production departments, and the resulting variances should not necessarily be interpreted as favorable or unfavorable without examining the effects of the substitution on the quantity variances.

Labor wage rate variance

Typically the variances resulting from budgeted and actual wage rates are very small, since labor costs can be forecast with greater accuracy than materials costs. Among the factors which might lead to significant labor rate variances are:

1. Uncertainty about production levels and employee turnover, possibly resulting in the substitution of high-cost labor for less skilled employees for short periods of time.

2. Substantial use of unbudgeted overtime to meet unusually high demand.

3. The unexpected imposition of wage and price controls by the government, preventing scheduled salary raises from being implemented.

Most of the causes of a large labor rate variance are beyond the control of the individual responsible for hiring workers, and also most will be beyond the control of the factory foreman. Only when the variances are both large and persistent is it likely to be worthwhile to investigate.

Materials quantity variance

A large materials quantity variance could result from the substitution of low-grade material in a process requiring a higher grade, theft of raw materials, a major accident resulting in spoilage, or failure to observe strict production standards in the factory. All of these causes might be of concern to management and warrant investigation. The materials quantity variance will usually be reported to the production manager and/or the factory foreman on a routine basis, enabling him to closely monitor the input/output ratio in the factory.

Labor quantity variance

An abnormal labor usage variance could have origins similar to those of the materials quantity variance: labor "shirking," an accident requiring that work representing hours of labor be discarded or reworked, or the use of less (or more highly) skilled workers in a job not designed for their skill level. Large or persistent variances would probably trigger an investigation by management, otherwise they would simply be reported to the production manager or foreman.

SUMMARY

For the purposes of analyzing and controlling manufacturing performance, actual results must be compared to a set of standards. Variance analysis is a technique for systematically examining the results during a period against the expected results. A summary of the variances provides management with a quick means of identifying any departures from performance standards so that further investigation or correction may take place.

Most organizations prepare some form of periodic variance

summary, which provides the basis for a formal or informal review of operating results. Timely investigation of abnormal variances can mean substantial savings to a firm.

Chapter 7

Standard Costs for Overhead and Overhead Variance Analysis

STANDARD COSTS FOR OVERHEAD

Many modern organizations, in particular those in the service sector of the economy, are characterized by a cost structure in which direct labor and direct materials costs are relatively insignificant compared to indirect product costs. Thus controlling overhead is a major concern to managers. The technique of variance analysis can be extended to help management uncover the causes of discrepancies between actual and budgeted overhead costs.

The application of variance analysis to overhead requires a clear understanding of the behavior of total overhead costs with respect to production volume. Thus we begin with classification of the overhead costs into their fixed and variable components. (Review Chapters 2 and 3 at this point if you are uncertain about the distinction between fixed and variable overhead costs.) Budgeted overhead costs depend upon the level of fixed costs incurred by the firm as well as the anticipated production volume for the period; from the budgeted overhead costs and a measure of average production volume we may obtain a per unit overhead cost, known as the **standard overhead cost**. (Careful attention to the terms introduced in this chapter will eliminate much of the confusion which often accompanies overhead variance analysis.)

FLEXIBLE BUDGETS

Budgeted overhead costs are determined with the aid of what is referred to as a **flexible budget**, which expresses total overhead costs as a function of the expected volume of activity. The term flexible is used because the total overhead cost changes as the anticipated volume changes. A typical flexible budget is of the form:

$$\text{Total overhead cost} = FC + (VC) \times (\text{Number of units})$$

where FC is the total fixed cost and VC is the variable cost per unit.

The variable cost may be expressed in terms of units, labor hours, machine hours, or any other factor of production; the choice depends upon the historical behavior of the variable portion of overhead costs. If these costs increase in direct proportion to labor hours worked, we will use that as the multiplier instead of units of output. This decision may affect our breakdown of the overhead variance into its different components, a fact which will be explored further below.

THE HIGH-LOW METHOD OF DETERMINING FIXED COSTS

Sometimes it is difficult from a description of the costs to determine exactly how much of the total overhead costs are fixed and how much represent the variable portion. One method of handling this problem is the **high-low method**, which uses historical cost records to estimate the fixed cost of production. Assume that a firm has the following data on its overhead costs for the previous six months, and wants to prepare a flexible budget to improve planning for the current period.

Month	Total overhead cost ($)	Direct labor hours worked
July	2,600	1,600
August	2,810	1,850
September	3,150	2,200
October	3,400	2,400
November	2,860	1,900
December	3,000	2,100

The hi-low method uses the data from the months of highest and lowest activity in the flexible budget to infer the cost behavior at different production volumes. The following equations represent total overhead cost at the two production volumes:

October: $3,400 = FC + VC(2,400$ direct labor hours)
July: $2,600 = FC + VC(1,600$ direct labor hours)

Using the method of simultaneous equations, we subtract one from the other and get:

$800 = VC(800$ direct labor hours)

Thus variable cost per direct labor hour is $1.00. Substituting this into the flexible budget for either July or October, the fixed cost may also be calculated. In this case it is $1,000. This method, of course, is only an approximation of the breakdown of fixed and variable costs, and if other more reliable sources can be found for this information they should be used.

DETERMINATION OF STANDARD OVERHEAD COST

In Chapter 2, we discussed different allocation rates for overhead costs. In a standard costing system, one of these allocation bases will be selected and used in a flexible budget to determine the standard overhead cost, or burden rate, for the purpose of applying overhead to product units. Assume for now a firm has chosen as its allocation basis standard direct labor hours. A standard direct labor hour is the amount of time it should have taken on average to produce a certain output. It is not the same as an actual direct labor hour, which is the time it actually took during a specific period to produce a particular output. The firm chose this as its allocation basis because it has found in the past that overhead costs vary directly with the actual output (which may be expressed in standard direct labor hours) of the factory, not with the number of hours used to produce that output.

The firm's estimate of its production costs for a typical month are set out in the table below.

	Fixed ($)	Variable ($)
Indirect labor	20,000	40,000
Heat and light	2,000	10,000
Oil	0	10,000
Maintenance	6,000	8,000
Depreciation	5,000	0
Insurance	5,000	0
Taxes	8,000	3,000
Miscellaneous	2,000	1,000
Total	48,000	72,000

The firm's normal operating volume is 24,000 direct labor hours. **Normal volume** has a very specific meaning in this context: it is the expected long-run average production volume for the firm. Normal volume is usually calculated using a time horizon which covers a normal business cycle, and includes periods of exceptionally favorable operating conditions as well as exceptionally poor ones. Normal volume does not necessarily mean the volume at which the firm expects to operate in the immediate future; due to fluctuations in product demand or raw materials prices, a firm may deliberately plan to operate at greater than normal volume in one period, and less than normal volume in another. The long-run average will smooth out these differences over time.

Most firms use normal volume to calculate their standard overhead cost. Normal volume is used so that the standard overhead cost does not reflect temporary fluctuations in production volume. In the case of the firm in our example, this would mean using 24,000 direct labor hours as the basis for allocating the total overhead costs. The standard overhead cost may be found using the flexible budget, and dividing both sides by the normal volume to get the standard overhead cost per direct labor hour.

$$\text{Standard overhead cost} = \frac{\$48,000 + \$72,000}{24,000 \text{ d.l.h.}}$$

This should look very familiar by now. Recall that we found the overhead application rate (OAR) in Chapter 2 in an identical way. The only difference between this process and what was done in Chapter 2 is that now we are using budgeted costs and normal operating volume as the basis for calculating the overhead application rate, to facilitate the analysis of overhead variances.

CALCULATING OVERHEAD VARIANCES

The illustration of overhead variance calculation will be accomplished by using data on the Daley Company given below. The data on the overhead costs for the period are as follows:

	Budgeted ($)	Actual ($)	Applied ($)
Variable factory overhead	21,000	20,274	
Fixed factory overhead	14,000	14,061	
Total	35,000	34,335	32,700

The total overhead variance, $2,300, is the difference between actual overhead costs and the amount of overhead applied. In this case it is favorable. Management, however, would like a more detailed breakdown of the difference between the actual amount of overhead costs incurred and the total amount of overhead applied to or absorbed by the product manufactured during the period in order to ascertain its origins.

Among the possible sources of the overhead variance are the following:

1. The overhead costs rose above their budgeted amounts; for example, the wage rate paid to indirect laborers was more than anticipated, or an insurance premium was unexpectedly increased.

2. The number of direct labor hours used to produce the period's output was greater than the standard number of direct labor hours; that is, there was an increase in overhead costs due to inefficiency on the part of the labor force in the factory.

3. The actual production volume for the period was lower than that used in determining the standard overhead rate; that is, the firm was not operating at normal volume.

Each of these sources of overhead variance will be explored further below. First the flexible budget for the factory overhead must be determined from the information given. We will assume that the Daley Company's budget for the period reflects normal volume, that is for this period the company planned to operate at its long-run average production volume. The information on budgeted production volume is in Figure 12.

As may be seen, the budgeted volume for the period is 700 units, and the standard direct labor hours needed to produce that number of units are 3,500 (0.5 hours×7,000 units). The budgeted overhead costs, at a volume of 7,000 units, are $14,000 fixed and $21,000 variable. Using the method we illustrated in the previous section, we can find the stan-

	Budgeted production information
Units	7,000
Standard direct labor hours per unit	0.50
Fixed overhead	$14,000
Variable overhead per unit	$3.00

Figure 12. Daley Company budget

dard overhead cost by inserting these figures into the flexible budget:

$$\text{Standard overhead cost} = \frac{\$14,000 + \$21,000}{3,500 \text{ standard d.l.h.}}$$

Thus the standard overhead cost per standard direct labor hour is $10.00. Note that we have used the word standard in describing both the overhead cost and the direct labor hours. The firm will absorb $10.00 of overhead for each standard direct labor hour worked; a standard direct labor hour is the number of hours it should have taken to produce a given amount of output. Thus even if it took 0.6 hours to produce one unit, only $5.00 of overhead will be applied, since only standard direct labor hours are required to produce one unit of output. Overhead absorption rates always use a standard unit of measure as the allocation basis, primarily because it makes internal record-keeping simpler, and because it gives a more accurate estimate of the long-run average production cost.

LEVEL OF DETAIL IN OVERHEAD VARIANCE ANALYSIS

Overhead variances may be calculated using a three-variance analysis or a two-variance analysis technique. A three-variance analysis is generally used when it is believed that overhead costs vary with production inputs, not production outputs. Thus if fuel for a generator was the major component of the manufacturing cost, and the generator was used continually in the manufacturing process, then overhead costs would vary with the number of machine hours used, not with the actual units produced. If an entire lot of widgets had to be rejected because they did not meet specifications, the overhead costs for the period would still be high, because the generator had to be run consistently to produce them. Thus in this case overhead would vary with inputs, not outputs, of the production process.

If, on the other hand, the major component of overhead cost was for temporary packaging for finished but undistributed products, then this cost would vary with output, not with input. Inefficient use of labor or materials in the actual manufacturing process would not increase the amount of packaging material used, and therefore there would be no overhead variance associated with production efficiency. In this case a two-variance analysis would furnish management with all the information it needed.

Both a two-variance and a three-variance analysis yield the same total variance; they must, by definition. The only difference is in the breakdown of the total variance into its separate components. A two-variance analysis provides a breakdown of the total overhead variance into two components:

1. Spending variance

2. Volume variance

A three-variance analysis provides the following breakdown of the total variance:

1. Spending variance

2. Efficiency variance

3. Volume variance

The relationship between the variances resulting from a two-variance analysis and a three-variance analysis is shown in Figure 13.

EXPLANATION OF OVERHEAD VARIANCES

The spending variance is that amount of the total overhead variance originating in a change in the standard costs used in the flexible budget. For example, if fixed costs in the flexible budget are estimated to be $10,000, and a taxing authority imposes a tax surcharge of $100, the actual fixed costs will increase by that amount. Or suppose the variable overhead cost assumes a cost per kilowatt hour for electricity of $0.14, which is raised during the accounting period to $0.15. Both increased costs will be reflected in the spending variance. (Of course, any change in the standard cost of overhead components which is not temporary should prompt management to change the flexible budget for future periods.) The spending variance reflects both price changes and increased or decreased resource use not attributable to other causes, i.e., the efficiency variance or the volume variance. A large spending variance would need to be investigated in greater detail to determine the underlying problems.

The efficiency variance is the amount by which variance overhead costs are increased by decreased efficiency in the

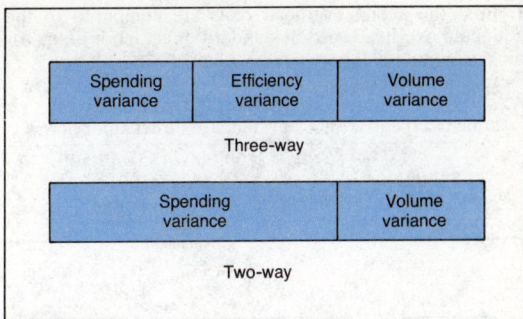

Figure 13. Relationship between two-way and three-way variance analysis

manufacturing process, or vice versa. If there is a lot of wasted labor time, and overhead increases with labor input rather than production output, a certain amount of overhead variance will be due to labor inefficiency. In a two-way variance analysis the efficiency variance is not calculated as it is believed that there is no change in overhead costs due to labor efficiency.

The volume variance is the difference between actual overhead costs and absorbed overhead costs due to a change from the budgeted production volume. Recall that the amount of overhead applied to each unit is determined using normal volume as the estimated volume. If the firm does not produce at that level during a given period, the total amount of fixed costs absorbed will be more or less than the budgeted fixed costs. This difference is the under- or over-absorbed fixed overhead, and is referred to as the volume variance.

TWO-WAY VARIANCE ANALYSIS

Assume the following information for a firm for the month of May. The firm budgets overhead as follows:

Total overhead=$100,000+$5×Standard direct labor hours

Its normal volume is 50,000 standard direct labor hours a month. For the month of May the firm has recorded $360,000 in actual overhead costs, and 49,000 actual direct labor hours. The output produced was equivalent to 49,500 standard direct labor hours. (Note that this implies that labor was marginally more efficient than expected during the period, producing more units in 49,000 hours than the standard called for.)

A two-way variance is calculated using the technique outlined in Figure 14. Applying the formula to the information in the example above, the variances are calculated in three steps below.

1. First the actual overhead costs are compared to the budgeted overhead costs at standard direct labor hours for the period to find the spending variance.

Actual overhead costs	Budgeted overhead costs at standard direct labor hours
$360,000	$100,000+($5×49,500)$347,500
	$12,500 Spending variance unfavorable

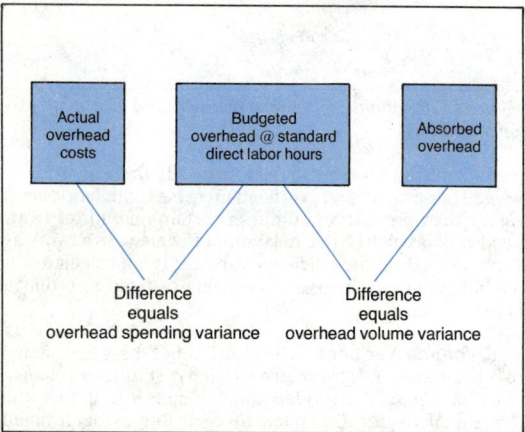

Figure 14. Two-way variance analysis

This is a rather large spending variance (nearly 4%) for the firm, and might trigger an investigation by management.

2. Next the standard overhead cost, or the overhead allocation rate, must be found using the firm's flexible budget. This is the amount of overhead which will be applied to units of output, in this case expressed in standard direct labor hours.

$$\frac{\text{Total overhead costs at normal volume}}{\text{Normal volume}}=\text{Standard overhead cost}$$

$$\frac{\$100,000+(\$5\times50,000)}{50,000}=\$7.00 \text{ per standard d.l.h.}$$

3. The volume variance is found by comparing the budgeted overhead at standard direct labor hours, found by using the flexible budget, to the absorbed overhead at standard direct labor hours, using the standard overhead cost. The flexible budget provides a realistic estimate of overhead costs in relation to the production volume, since the total overhead cost is expressed as a function of production volume. Comparing this to the absorbed overhead gives an estimate of how much of the budgeted overhead costs were not absorbed due to the decreased production volume in the period. The volume variance of $1,000 is the underabsorbed fixed overhead, and is entirely due to the departure from normal production volume. Another way to put it is that the company spent $1,000 to generate production capacity which it did not use during the period.

Another way to find the volume variance is by taking the fixed cost absorption rate and multiplying by the difference between standard direct labor hours for the period and normal direct labor hours. The fixed cost absorption rate is the part of the total absorption rate which is from fixed costs, or in this case $7 minus the variable cost of $5 per standard direct labor hour. The normal volume is 50,000 hours, and the volume for the period was 49,500 standard direct labor hours. This difference, 500 hours, times the fixed cost absorption rate of $2, is $1,000, the volume variance.

Budgeted overhead at standard direct labor hours	Absorbed overhead
$100,000+($5×49,500)	($7×49,500)
$347,500	$346,500
$1,000 volume variance unfavorable	

The total unfavorable overhead variance of $14,500 has been broken down into two smaller variances, an unfavorable spending variance of $12,500 and an unfavorable volume variance of $1,000. *Note that the number of actual direct labor hours used during the period is not used in the calculation of a two-way variance.*

THREE-WAY VARIANCE ANALYSIS

The chart on the following page shows the method for calculating the three-way variance.

Assume the firm in the example above budgets its overhead for the period using the following flexible budget:

Total overhead=fixed overhead+($5×actual direct labor hours)

It expects overhead costs to increase with the labor input, rather than the manufacturing output, as in the previous illustration of the two-way variance. The use of actual direct labor hours in the flexible budget indicates that management would find the information in a three-way variance analysis useful, since it is expected that overhead costs will vary with labor efficiency. The calculation of three variances is demonstrated in four steps below.

1. Spending variance is found by comparing actual overhead costs with budgeted overhead costs at actual direct labor hours.

Actual overhead costs	Budgeted overhead at actual direct labor hours
	$100,000+($5×49,000)
$360,000	$345,000
$15,000 spending variance unfavorable	

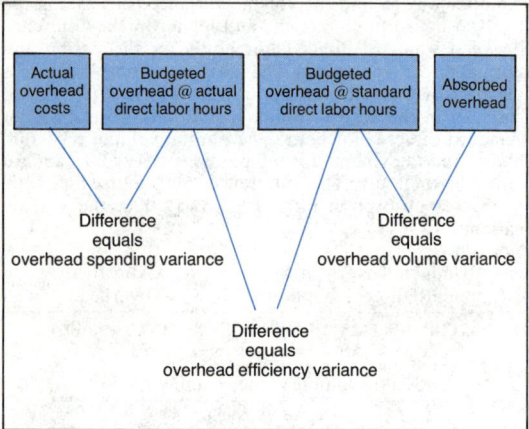

Figure 15. Three-way overhead variance analysis

2. The efficiency variance is found by comparing the budgeted overhead at actual direct labor hours to the budgeted overhead at the standard direct labor hours. The difference in these two represents the amount by which overhead is expected to have changed due to the increased labor efficiency.

Budgeted overhead at actual direct labor hours	Budgeted overhead at standard direct labor hours
$100,000+($5×49,000)	$100,000+($5×49,500)
$345,000	$347,500
$2,500 efficiency variance favorable	

3. The overhead absorption rate, or standard overhead cost, is found by using the flexible budget to calculate the total overhead cost at normal volume. This will be the same overhead absorption rate used in the two-variance analysis above.

$$\frac{\text{Total overhead cost at normal volume}}{\text{Normal volume}} = \frac{\$100,000+(\$5×50,000)}{50,000} = \$7 \text{ per standard direct labor hour}$$

4. Volume variance is the difference between budgeted overhead at standard direct labor hours and absorbed overhead. Volume variance will be the same as that calculated in the two-way variance above, since the difference in budgeted overhead at standard direct labor hours and absorbed overhead is the same.

Budgeted overhead at standard direct labor hours	Absorbed overhead
$100,000+($5\times49,500)$	$7\times49,500$
$347,500	$346,500
$1,000 volume variance unfavorable	

Comparing the variances from the two- and three-way analyses, we can see that it is the level of detail which changes, not the total variance.

	Two-way	Three-way
Spending variance	12,000 U	15,000 U
Efficiency variance	0	2,500 F
Volume variance	1,000 U	1,000 U
Total variance	13,500 U	13,500 U

REPORTING THE VARIANCES

Overhead variances are more difficult to interpret than direct labor and direct materials variances, since they result from a combination of many different factors. In general, the spending and efficiency variances would be the concern of the department head or factory manager, since these would be at least partly under her control. In many cases the spending variance would be broken down into price and quantity components, and the factory manager held responsible for only the quantity variable. The volume variance is not the responsibility of the plant manager, since production quotas are imposed from above, and thus she is not able to control the overhead variance due to volume changes. This variance would be reported to higher management, and only reported at the factory level in order to help the manager explain the total overhead variance to her superiors.

SUMMARY

Control of overhead costs is important to many organizations. Understanding the causes of divergences from budgeted costs is the first step in controlling those costs. Overhead variance analysis is a technique for breaking down the total variance into its individual components. Both two-way and three-way variance analyses are possible, and the choice depends on the expected behavior of overhead costs in relation to production inputs and production outputs.

Chapter 8

Capital Investment Appraisal

THE IMPORTANCE OF CAPITAL INVESTMENT DECISIONS

Capital investment is the investment of funds in assets which will provide a long-term benefit to an organization. Decisions about the acquisition of capital assets need particular attention, since they frequently involve the expenditure of large sums of money by an organization. Such decisions cannot easily or cheaply be reversed, and they often commit an organization to a certain type of activity for several years.

APPRAISAL METHODS: SOME GENERAL POINTS

When an organization makes a capital investment, it pays out cash today in the hope of receiving cash back in future years. An investment appraisal consists of comparing cash outflows now with cash inflows at a future date, and approval of the project depends on the amounts and timings of these cash flows.

The appraisal methods dealt with later are all variations on this same basic theme, albeit with differing degrees of sophistication. In fact it is very easy to jump from the first section to appraisal methods without giving due consideration to the practical difficulties of estimating the cash flows from a particular project. It must be recognized that in any investment appraisal the preparation of the estimates of inflows and outflows is a very time-consuming and imprecise exercise. In fact the practical problems in investment appraisal are mainly in the areas listed below, rather than in the application of the methods themselves.

Estimating demand, prices, rates of growth, etc., and the risk associated with each of these. This is particularly difficult where the project is completely new and comparisons with similar existing projects cannot be made. Also difficult is estimating the life of the assets (both technological and economic) and their residual values, assessing the potential output of plant facilities, their maintenance costs, etc., and attempting to evaluate any spin-off to other projects. Interdependence of projects, while common, does pose serious problems of cost estimation, such as estimating any changes in working capital requirements as a result of the implementation of a project.

THE TIME VALUE OF MONEY

The essence of capital investment appraisal is a comparison of present cash flows with cash flows of a later period. However, one dollar held now is not worth the same as one dollar receivable one year from now, because one dollar now could be invested to yield more than one dollar in the future. If, for example, the current rate of interest is 10%, a dollar held for one year would have accumulated ten cents

in interest by the end of the year. If this interest was reinvested with the principal, and held for another year, the
total would accumulate to $1.21 by the end of the second
year. This compounding process can be formalized as follows:

$1.00 now will accumulate to
$1.00 $(1+r)$ in one year
$1.00 $(1+r)$ $(1+r)$ in two years
$1.00 $(1+r)^n$ in n years
where r is the current rate of interest.

Using 10% as the interest rate the figures given earlier can
be confirmed.

$1.00 $(1+0.10)$ $=$1.10$
$1.00 (1.10) $(1.10)=$1.21$

Generalizing, we can say that $1.00 now will be worth $1.00
$(1+r)^n$ in n years. The value of $1.00 in n years is called the
future value of one dollar, and implies a specific period of
time and a specific rate of interest.

But what is $1.00 receivable in n years equivalent to now?
Formally, it is equivalent to $\frac{\$1.00}{(1+r)^n}$ now.

Using the above example (again assuming a 10% rate of
interest) this means that:

$1.00 receivable one year from now is worth $\frac{\$1.00}{(1.10)}=\$0.91$
today.

$1.00 receivable two years from now is worth $\frac{\$1.00}{(1.10)^2}=\$0.83$
today.

Put another way, the **present value** of $1.00 receivable one
year from now, assuming a 10% interest rate, is $0.91. The
calculation procedure is referred to as **discounting**. In
practice, present value tables (as well as future value tables)
are used to determine the appropriate discount factor, thus
eliminating the need for calculations of the type above.
(Present value tables may be found in Appendices 1 and 2.)
Techniques of project evaluation which use discounted cash
flows explicitly incorporate the time value of money into the
appraisal. Two of these methods are introduced below,
along with a third, the payback period, which does not make
use of discounted cash flows.

TECHNIQUES OF INVESTMENT APPRAISAL

A number of appraisal methods are found in practice. The
most frequently used methods are the payback period, the
internal rate of return (IRR) and the net present value
(NPV). Although the last method is theoretically superior
to the others, it is not always preferred by managers.

Payback Period

Basically this method is concerned with identifying the time
taken to recover the amount originally invested in a project.
The decision rule associated with the method is to select the
project with the shortest payback period.

Example:

The net cash flows for three projects are estimated as follows:

Project	Year	0	1	2	3	4	5
A		(10,000)	2,000	2,000	2,000	4,000	6,000
B		(10,000)	5,000	3,000	2,000	2,000	0
C		(10,000)	1,000	1,000	8,000	2,000	0

The payback period is four years for project A and three
years for projects B and C. Using the payback period as the
criterion for evaluation, either B or C should be undertaken
in preference to A. The payback method has the following
advantages:

It is easy to calculate. It tends to eliminate high-risk
projects, where risk is associated with the uncertainty of
future events. It emphasizes short- and medium-term liquidity.

On the other hand, it can be seen that there are certain
disadvantages with the method:

1. It ignores all cash flows after the payback period, thus
putting long-lived projects at a disadvantage. Such projects
may well be the most profitable, when evaluated using a
discounted cash flow technique, as will be demonstrated
below.

2. It does not take into account the time value of money.
(For example, see projects B and C above. The cash flows
from project B occur earlier than those from C, but the two
are ranked equally in terms of payback period.)

When used in isolation, the payback period may lead to
suboptimal decisions. When used in conjunction with other
methods it serves a useful purpose, particularly in providing
a measure of risk.

Discounted cash flow techniques

The main advantages of discounted cash flow techniques
over the payback period method are that they do take into
account the time value of money, and they include all cash
flows in the calculations. Two methods are commonly used,
the net present value and internal rate of return.

Net present value

This method discounts all cash flows to present values, at
some predetermined rate of interest (the discount rate). In

general, the discount rate used will be the cost of capital to
the organization, adjusted for the expected risk of the project (see section on risk and uncertainty). The present value
of the outflows is then deducted from the present value of
the cash inflows, to arrive at a net present value of the
project. If the NPV is positive the project is accepted. If it is
negative the project is rejected.

Example:

The cash flows associated with project A are estimated to be
as follows:

Year	0	1	2	3	4	5
Cash flows	(10,000)	2,000	2,000	2,000	4,000	6,000

The cost of capital to the firm is 10%.

The cash flows are discounted and summed as follows:

Year	Cash flow	Discount factor	Present value
0	(10,000)	1.00	(10,000)
1	2,000	0.91	1,820
2	2,000	0.83	1,660
3	2,000	0.75	1,500
4	4,000	0.68	2,720
5	6,000	0.62	3,720
		Net present value	1,420

Because the NPV is positive, the project should be
accepted. The rationale for the NPV method is that the
discounting process effectively allows for payment of interest on the money used to finance the project. An NPV of
zero means that the project could be financed from funds on
which interest has been paid (at the discount rate) and still
break even. A positive NPV means that a profit will be made
over and above any interest payments. A negative NPV
means that the interest payments would not be covered.

Internal rate of return:

The internal rate of return for a project is that discount rate
which when applied to the cash flows makes its NPV equal
to zero. The method requires several approximations to be
made before determining the precise return. (In practice
this will not be a problem since such calculations will almost
certainly be computerized.)

Example:

Calculate the IRR for Project A above. As a starting point
10% is used as before. This gives an NPV of $1,420, which in
turn indicates that the IRR is in excess of 10%. The process
is then repeated using a higher discount rate (say 16%). This
gives a negative NPV, indicating that the return is less than
16%.

Year	10% Cash flow	10% Discount factor	10% Present value	16% Discount factor	16% Present value
0	(10,000)	1.00	(10,000)	1.00	(10,000)
1	2,000	0.91	1,820	0.86	1,720
2	2,000	0.83	1,660	0.74	1,480
3	2,000	0.75	1,500	0.64	1,280
4	4,000	0.68	2,270	0.55	2,200
5	6,000	0.62	3,720	0.48	2,880
Net present value			1,420		(560)

By a process of further approximations the correct yield (IRR) can be calculated. For most purposes simple linear interpolations will give an approximate yield. The procedure for this is illustrated in Figure 16. The two NPVs are plotted against the discount rates. The point at which the line joining these (or extrapolated if necessary) cuts the NPV=0 axis gives the approximate yield. Further calculations would enable greater accuracy to be achieved. The yield thus calculated is then compared with the cost of capital or "cut-off" rate. If the yield exceeds the latter the project is accepted. If the cost of capital exceeds the yield, the project is rejected. If the cost of capital was 10% above, the project would be accepted.

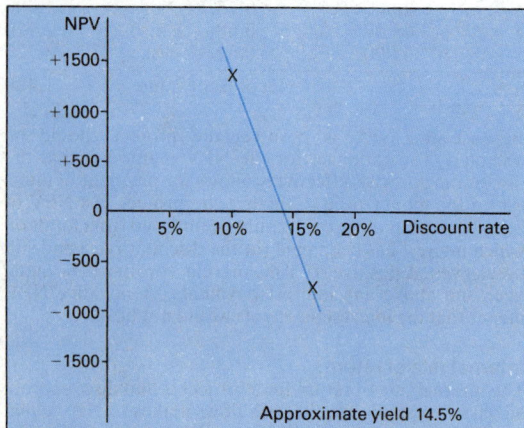

Figure 16. Linear approximation of yield

One particular problem associated with the yield method is that under certain circumstances it is possible to obtain more than one solution. Single solutions will only occur with so-called conventional cash flow patterns, namely net outflows followed by net inflows. If cash outflows are followed by inflows, which in turn are followed by outflows (such as might be associated with the oil industry), multiple solutions will be achieved. In fact with non-conventional cash flows it is possible to obtain one yield, multiple yields or no yield. This problem does not arise if one uses the NPV method.

A COMPARISON OF THE DISCOUNTED CASH FLOW METHODS

Both the NPV and the IRR methods have certain advantages and disadvantages associated with their use, and much has been written about them in recent years. Both methods have attracted support and criticism on theoretical and practical grounds. Net present value gives a consistently "correct" answer in all situations, but the IRR technique appears to be more readily understood by businessmen. For a simple accept-or-reject decision regarding a single project, both methods should give the same result, i.e., if the yield is greater than the cost of capital, the NPV would automatically be positive when cash flows are discounted at the cost of capital. There are, however, cases where a choice between alternative projects must be made, as with mutually exclusive projects.

Mutually exclusive projects

The situation frequently arises where several ways exist to solve a particular business problem. For example, two different manufacturing methods are available to produce the same output, or alternative advertising media are under consideration for a particular campaign. Each of these options can be viewed as a project. However, only one of these projects can be accepted. How, then, is a choice to be made between them? By way of illustration let us assume that there are two competing projects under consideration for a firm which has a 10% cost of capital:

Project	Cash flows Year 0	Cash flows Year 1	Net present value	Internal rate of return
A	(100,000)	125,000	13,750	25%
B	(200,000)	240,000	18,400	20%

The problem now becomes apparent. The yield and NPV approaches suggest different solutions. The reason for this is the size of the investment. The absolute size of the NPV is clearly greater for the larger project than for the smaller one, even though the rate of return is smaller. The project with the larger NPV should always be accepted over that with the smaller. To see the intuition behind this, it is very useful to consider the incremental cash flows for the mutually exclusive projects, to ascertain the internal rate of return on the excess investment. The incremental cash flows are the extra cash expenditures and receipts associated with the larger project. From this comparison it will become apparent that the extra investment still yields in excess of the cost of capital.

Project	A	B	Incremental cash flows
Cash outflow	100	200	100
Cash inflow	125	240	115

The incremental IRR is 15%; the incremental NPV is
$4,650. This approach should make it clear that the addi-
tional investment required by project B has an IRR greater
than the firm's cost of capital.

The essential difference between NPV and yield

Both the NPV and yield method make implicit assumptions
about the rate of return on cash flows reinvested. Effectively
the yield method assumes that cash reinvested in the course
of the life of a project earns at the same rate as the rest of the
project. The NPV method assumes that the re-investment
rate is the same as the discount rate used, namely the cost of
capital or cut-off rate. The justification for either assumption is questionable, and dual rate calculations are made by
some organizations.

RISK AND UNCERTAINTY

The discussion to date has been based on the assumption
that the cash flows to be used in the appraisal methods can
be ascertained with certainty. In reality such precision does
not exist, and decisions must be made on less than perfect
information. To date no completely satisfactory method of
dealing with risk and uncertainty has been devised, but a
number of techniques have been developed which provide
insight into the problem. These are dealt with below. These
techniques have not been developed in a particularly sys-
tematic way, and management must consider its attitudes
toward risk, and attempt to develop sensible criteria for
incorporating risk into the decision process. Typically management should ask:

1. What is the expected value of a project?
2. What are the possible outcomes that might result?
3. What are the risks associated with the possible outcomes?
4. Is it possible to reduce the risk associated with the project
by diversification?
5. What is the relationship between possible returns and the
levels of risk associated with the project?

Shortened payback period

The payback method, by focusing attention on shorter lives,
tends to lead to investments being chosen which have a
relatively small risk of loss. For more risky projects shorter
payback periods are sometimes required. All of the problems associated with payback remain, but the risk of significant loss is considerably reduced.

Higher discount rate

It is quite common for management to decide that a higher
rate of return is needed on certain projects to cover the
perceived extra risk involved in the project. Such a method
is simple, and is of particular use where probabilities cannot
be accurately established for the returns expected. It has the
disadvantage of confusing the discount factor, which takes
into account the time value of money, with the risk premium.

The use of probabilities

In the earlier sections it became clear that the discounted cash flow techniques were concerned with finding the NPV of projects. In choosing between projects the general aim was to determine the group of projects which gave the highest NPV. However, where risk is involved it is no longer clear exactly what the NPV of a project is. The outcomes of a risky project are by their very nature uncertain, and many possible outcomes exist. How, then, is the expected value of a project to be calculated?

For some projects, returns are so uncertain that management can do little more than guess at the outcomes. Even in this case the estimation of "most likely," "optimistic," and "pessimistic" outcomes can be very useful. Nonetheless, such projects pose very significant problems of analysis. For other projects it is possible to estimate the likely dispersion of outcomes, and to attach probabilities to these outcomes.

Example:

A company is considering investment in project X, which involves the production and sale of a new product at a selling price of $2 per unit and a manufacturing cost of $1 per unit. The cost of the new machinery for the project is $10,000. There is some doubt as to the expected sales volume, and a study of the market has suggested the following probabilities:

Sales volume	Probability
2,000	0.1
3,000	0.3
4,000	0.4
5,000	0.2

The project will last for four years. The cost of capital is 10%. What is the expected NPV?

To answer this question, first calculate the cash flows for different sales volumes as in the table below:

Sales volume	Price per unit	Sales revenue ($)	Production costs ($)	Cash flows ($)
2,000	2	4,000	2,000	2,000
3,000	2	6,000	3,000	3,000
4,000	2	8,000	4,000	4,000
5,000	2	10,000	5,000·	5,000

Four possible NPVs can then be calculated:

($)

1. NPV given sales of 2,000 units.

Present value of cash outflows at time zero:	(10,000)
Present value of annuity of $2,000 for four years discounted at 10%	6,360
Net present value	(3,640)

2. NPV given sales of 3,000 units.

Present value of cash outflows at time zero:	(10,000)
Present value of annuity of $3,000 for four years discounted at 10%:	9,540
Net present value	(460)

3. NPV given sales of 4,000 units.

Present value of cash outflows at time zero:	(10,000)
Present value of annuity of $4,000 for four years discounted at 10%:	12,720
Net present value	2,720

4. NPV given sales of 5,000 units.

Present value of cash outflows at time zero:	(10,000)
Present value of annuity of $5,000 for four years discounted at 10%	15,900
Net present value	5,900

These can be summarized as follows:

NPV ($)	Probability	NPV ×probability ($)
(3,640)	0.1	(364)
(460)	0.3	(138)
2,720	0.4	1,088
5,900	0.2	1,180
Expected value		1,766

In fact, one figure for expected sales could have been used, based on the same averaging process, to give the same result.

The main **advantage** of expected value is that it does provide a single estimate of project value. However, the use of such an averaging process does introduce problems. First, the expected value, as it is calculated as a mean, does not necessarily point to the most likely result, and management may be more interested in this latter figure. In the above example the most likely result is an NPV of $2,720, with a probability of achievement of 0.4 or 40%. It is also possible for an expected value to be calculated which is not a possible result but merely an average of two or more quite different possibilities.

The techniques of capital investment appraisal provide management with the means of comparing risky alternatives regardless of the timing of the associated cash flows. Although the analysis cannot provide a full appraisal of the costs and benefits of different strategies (since certain of

these may be intangible or unquantifiable), it can focus
management's attention on those outcomes which can be
anticipated and help them to select from among competing
projects.

Chapter 9

Allocating Service Department Costs

In Chapter 2, we discussed the determination of product cost for a simple factory using a full costing system. Most firms have more complicated organization structures, however, with one or more service centers providing services to other departments, or support centers, or acting in an administrative capacity or providing facilities to other departments. A department in which actual manufacturing or production takes place is referred to as a **production center**; the costs of the service and support centers are frequently assigned to the production centers by means of an **interdepartmental allocation rate**, which is simply another kind of overhead rate.

TYPES OF SERVICE CENTERS

Some typical examples of service and support centers, the costs of which would be allocated to one or more of the cost centers, are listed below.

> Personnel
> Purchasing
> Receiving
> Maintenance
> Production scheduling
> Accounting
> Building services

As is evident from this list, these departments share the characteristic that they do not produce any products for ultimate sale to the customer. Note that there are a number of significant omissions from the list: specifically, selling, distribution, and administration centers. As pointed out in Chapter 2, these costs are traditionally treated as **period costs** and expensed directly onto the income statement each accounting period.

There are several reasons why management might want to allocate the costs of the departments listed above to cost centers rather than treating them as period costs like selling, distribution and administrative costs. Among these reasons are the following:

1. Since these are necessary product costs, they should be reflected in the inventory cost, and expensed onto the income statement as part of the cost of goods sold. Thus the internal accounting system can provide directly the information required for external financial reporting.

2. For decision-making purposes, inclusion of the service center costs in the product cost gives a more accurate estimate of the total production cost.

3. For the purpose of cost control, allocation of a service center cost to a department using that service will encourage the manager of the latter to make rational decisions regarding its use; that is, cost allocation will help to prevent waste or abuse of the internal services provided.

4. The calculation of cost-based prices for reimbursement purposes requires information on the full cost of the products which therefore should include service center costs.

ALLOCATION PROCEDURES

Interdepartmental cost allocation generally is accomplished using one of three procedures:

1. One-step allocation
2. Sequential or step-down allocation
3. Simultaneous allocation

The first method, simultaneous allocation, is used when service departments do not provide any services to each other, or when the cost of such cross-services is negligible. In that case the service center costs can be apportioned directly among the cost centers without any intermediate allocations. The diagram in Figure 17 shows an organization with this structure; the personnel and maintenance departments each provide services to the production department, but do not exchange any services directly with each other.

The second method is used when service centers do provide services to each other, as well as to the production centers, but it is possible to trace the flow of services in one direction. An example might be a firm with three service centers: personnel, purchasing and maintenance. Personnel supplies purchasing, purchasing supplies services to maintenance, and in addition each of them provides services to the production

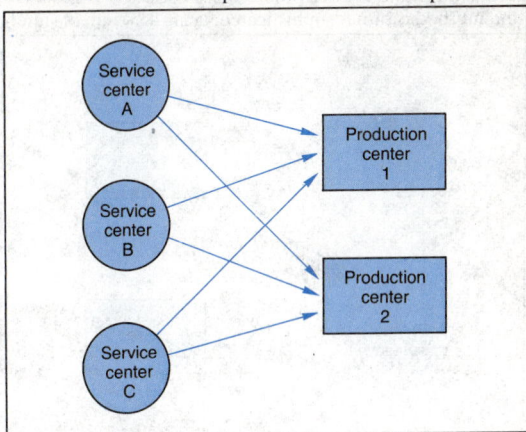

Figure 17. Organization structure suitable for one-step allocation

centers. Figure 18 illustrates this situation. The objective of
the allocation method in these circumstances would be to
apportion the personnel department's costs among the purchasing and production departments, assign the purchasing
department's costs to maintenance and the production centers, and finally apportion the maintenance costs among the
two production centers. The sequential allocation process
will be illustrated in detail below.

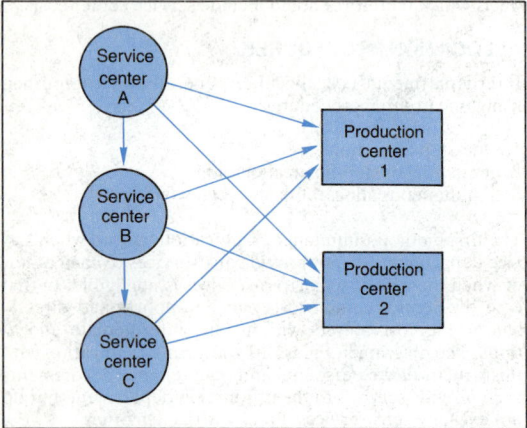

Figure 18. Organization suitable for step-down allocation

The third method, simultaneous or cross-allocation, is used
when service departments provide mutual services as well as
services to production centers. An example might be a
consulting firm with two divisions and two service centers,
personnel and copying, which provide services to the consulting units and to each other, as in Figure 19. This allocation method is rather sophisticated, using a system of simul-

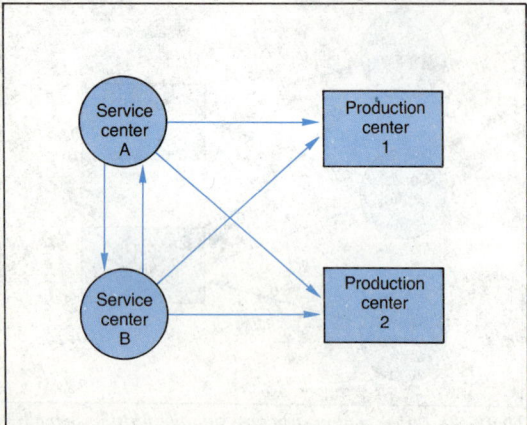

Figure 19. Organization suitable for simultaneous allocation

taneous equations, and the step-down allocation is frequently used in place of it. We will not illustrate its use here; an advanced text may be consulted for an explanation of the procedure.

ILLUSTRATION OF ALLOCATION PROCEDURES

A one-step allocation system is very simple to understand and implement, but it rarely provides the level of detail required by most organizations. The organization structure outlined in Figure 17 is not usually observed in a firm, and therefore a step-down or simultaneous allocation system is used, either because the organization structure requires it or because the cost of installing a more sophisticated system is not justified by the corresponding benefits.

Assume a firm has the following budgeted costs in its two service centers, the maintenance department and the purchasing department. It has two production centers in its factory, to which all service center costs will be allocated.

	Maintenance ($)	Purchasing ($)
Direct costs:		
Labor	9,000	3,000
Supplies	7,000	500
Indirect costs:		
Rent	400	420
Heat and light	100	80
Total	16,500	4,000

The two production departments manufacture two different items, with the following manufacturing data:

	Production Department A	Production Department B
Units	1,000	1,000
Direct labor hours	1,000	4,000
Machine hours	1,800	1,200
Direct materials cost	$80,000	$20,000

A decision must be made as to what allocation basis to use for apportioning the service center costs to the two production departments: this apportionment should reflect the relative intensity of use of the services by the production departments. A direct measure is not always available. For example, hours spent by the maintenance department in the two production departments would be the best allocation basis for maintenance cost, but a statistic of this sort is rarely recorded within an organization. Among the available alternatives, the choice of allocation basis may be made on the basis of the historical relationship between maintenance cost and manufacturing data, or by simple common sense.

Using machine hours as the allocation basis, the total maintenance costs, $16,500, would be assigned to the production departments as follows:

Department A	Department B
$16,500 \times \dfrac{180}{300} = \$9,900$	$16,500 \times \dfrac{120}{300} = \$6,600$

The amount of total maintenance costs which would be assigned to each unit of output manufactured in each of the two departments would be as follows:

Department A	Department B
$\dfrac{\$9,900}{1,000 \text{ units}} = \$9.90$	$\dfrac{\$6,600}{1,000 \text{ units}} = \$6.60$

The costs of the purchasing department must also be allocated between departments A and B. Assuming that direct material cost is most closely correlated with the total costs of the purchasing department over time (if the data were available, of course, this could be verified), the allocation would be made as follows:

Department A	Department B
$\$4,000 \times \dfrac{80,000}{100,000} = \$3,200$	$\$4,000 \times \dfrac{20,000}{100,000} = \$800$

On a per unit basis, the purchasing department costs would be assigned to the products as follows:

Department A	Department B
$\dfrac{\$3,200}{1,000} = \$3.20$	$\dfrac{\$800}{1,000} = \$0.80$

Step-down allocation

Assume a university has three service centers which provide services to each of its "production centers." The three service centers are Personnel, which is responsible for hiring all non-faculty personnel in the university; Buildings and Grounds, which maintains the physical plant of the university; and the Registrar, which is responsible for all billing procedures and which maintains files on the status of all students in the university. The production centers are the College and the Graduate School. The two departments are considered cost centers for the purpose of budgeting, and all costs are to be assigned ultimately to them.

Since Personnel supplies services to the Registrar, to Buildings and Grounds as well as to the College and Graduate School, its costs will be allocated first. Allocation bases must be determined for each set of costs to be allocated. For the sake of the example, we will assume the following allocation bases have been chosen on the basis of historical cost patterns.

Department	Allocation basis
Personnel	Number of employees
Buildings and Grounds	Square feet occupied
Registrar	Number of students enrolled

The data on the costs of each department and the resources employed is given in the chart below:

Department	Budgeted costs	Employees	Square feet	Students
Personnel	$350,000	–	–	–
Buildings and Grounds	$700,000	10	–	–
Registrar	$800,000	15	20,000	–
College	$14,000,000	20	250,000	2,000
Graduate School	$32,000,000	25	430,000	5,000

A step-down allocation proceeds by allocating the costs of one department at a time to those remaining. This is the reason that it is an inappropriate method when significant costs are incurred by departments that serve each other. We have assumed that such costs are negligible for the university in our example. The allocation then begins with the costs of the personnel department, which are assigned to the other four departments on the basis of the number of employees. (All allocations are rounded to the nearest thousand dollars.)

Department	Number of employees	Costs assigned ($)	Total costs ($)
Buildings and Grounds	10	50,000	750,000
Registrar	15	75,000	875,000
College	20	100,000	14,100,000
Graduate School	25	125,000	32,125,000

The costs of the personnel department were apportioned among the four other departments on the basis of the number of employees (non-faculty appointments) serving in each. The underlying assumption is that the costs of the personnel department increase with the total number of employees in the university, and each department should bear its part of those costs. For example, the buildings and grounds service center, with ten employees, was assigned one-seventh of the total costs of the personnel department.

Once the costs of the personnel department have been assigned, the total costs of the buildings and grounds service center are to be allocated among the remaining three departments. Note that the total costs of the buildings and grounds service center have been increased by $50,000, due to the personnel department costs assigned to it. These costs will be reallocated with the rest of the costs of buildings and grounds, in the "step-down" process. The allocation of the building and grounds costs takes place using square feet occupied as the allocation basis.

Department	Square feet	Costs assigned ($)	Total costs ($)
Registrar	20,000	21,000	896,000
College	250,000	268,000	14,368,000
Graduate School	430,000	461,000	32,586,000

Finally, the costs of the Registrar are allocated to the two remaining cost centers, the College and the Graduate School, on the basis of the number of students enrolled.

Department	Students	Costs assigned ($)	Total costs ($)
College	2,000	256,000	14,624,000
Graduate School	5,000	640,000	33,226,000

The total costs of the three service centers have now been assigned to the two "production centers" according to an estimate of their relative use of the service department resources.

If all the service departments in the university were included in the allocation procedure, the final costs assigned to the College and the Graduate School would represent a reasonable estimate of the total cost of educating a student. Obviously it would be only an approximation, since it is impossible to associate specific service costs with students, as is the case with all types of overhead costs.

These allocations may provide the basis for determining tuition costs, to predict the economic effects of new administrative policies, and possibly to motivate administrators to control the use of service center costs in their own departments. The usefulness of such an allocation system depends both on the rationality of the underlying assumptions and the purposes to which the allocation system is put.

Chapter 10

Profit Analysis

The overall function of any accounting system is to keep management fully informed about the profit performance of the firm as a whole and its various divisions. In Chapter 6 we discussed variance analysis as a technique for presenting information about cost control to management; here we will extend that technique to the analysis of profit performance.

THE UNDERLYING CAUSES OF PROFIT VARIANCE

Actual profits may be more or less than budgeted profits in a given period for a number of reasons, which may be grouped under "revenue" factors and "cost" factors. Changes in revenues arise for any or all of three reasons:

1. Actual sales volume different from budgeted sales volume;
2. Actual sales price different from budgeted sales price;
3. Actual sales mix (i.e., ratio of units of product A to units of Product B sold) different from budgeted sales mix.

The cost factors are analogous to the revenue factors:

1. If the sales volume was different than planned, and production volume was changed correspondingly, then the unit cost would vary due to the proportional change in fixed cost per unit;
2. The actual manufacturing cost per unit might be different than the budgeted cost;
3. The product mix might be different than planned, causing the total cost of goods sold to differ from the budgeted amount.

Analyzing the effect of each of these changes on the firm's total profits will be illustrated in turn.

We will begin with the simple case of showing a change in the gross margin of a single product company (therefore there will be no effects attributable to changes in product mix) due to a change first in unit price, then in sales volume. We will use variable costing in the analysis, thereby eliminating the fixed cost absorption rate as a source of variance in the gross margin.

The following information pertains to the Twain Company for the month of April:

	Budgeted ($)	Actual ($)	Variance ($)	
Sales revenue	20,000	21,600	1,600	Favorable
Cost of goods sold	12,000	11,700	1,500	Favorable
Gross margin	8,000	9,900	1,900	Favorable

The firm also had access to the following data on selling prices and volume:

	Budgeted	Actual
Number of units	10,000	9,000
Price per unit	$2.00	$2.40
Variable cost per unit	$1.20	$1.30
Contribution margin per unit	$0.80	$1.10

The company had an overall positive profit variance of $1,900, but management would like to know how much is attributable to each revenue factor and each cost factor.

SALES VOLUME VARIANCE

The sales volume variance is simply the change in profits due to a change in sales volume. It is computed as the budgeted sales volume times the standard contribution margin per unit minus the actual sales volume times the standard contribution margin per unit, as shown in Figure 20 below.

Using the data on the Twain Company for the month of April, we find an unfavorable volume variance of $800.

10,000	9,000
×$0.80	×$0.80
$8,000	$7,200

$800 unfavorable

Note that this amount is solely attributable to the change in the number of units sold, without reflecting the change in profit from any other source.

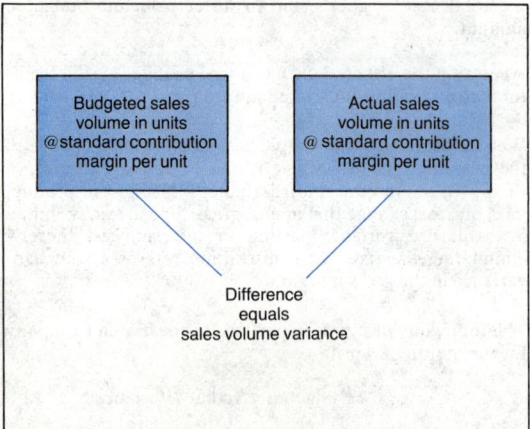

Figure 20. Sales volume variance for a single product

SALES PRICE VARIANCE

The sales price variance for the Twain Company may be

computed as in Figure 21. For the Twain Company, we get:

9,000	9,000
×$2.00	×$2.40
$18,000	$21,600

$3,600 favorable

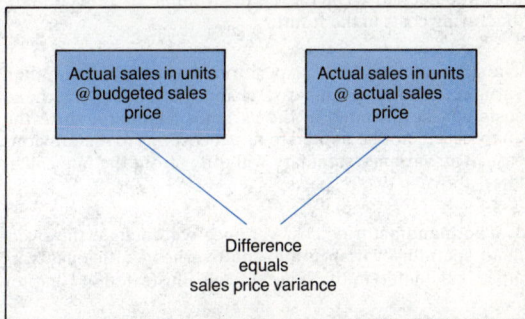

Figure 21. Sales price variance for a single product

The $3,600 is the change in profit that is due entirely to the price change, after eliminating the volume effects.

MANUFACTURING COST VARIANCE

Since we are using variable costing in this analysis, any change in the cost of goods sold for the Twain Company may be attributed entirely to a change in the unit variable cost. (For this kind of profit analysis, management usually does not break down the manufacturing cost variance into its specific components; a single figure is generally reported. The direct labor variances, direct materials variances, and variable portion of the overhead variance might be detailed in a separate schedule, although it is unlikely. Top management would in most cases not be interested in the detail of the manufacturing cost variances, and would delegate that authority to divisional or operating executives.)

The manufacturing cost variance, then, is the difference between the budgeted and actual variable cost per unit times the actual sales volume.

For the Twain Company, this amount is:

$1.20	$1.30
×9,000	×9,000
10,800	11,700

$900 unfavorable

Consolidating the information yields the following schedule of variances:

Sales volume variance	$800	unfavorable
Sales price variance	3,600	favorable
Manufacturing cost variance	900	unfavorable
Total variance	1,900	favorable

The total variance, $1,900, is the same as that reported on the first page of the chapter. It is now apparent, however, that the favorable variance is entirely attributable to the increase in sales price from $2.00 to $2.40. With the additional information supplied by the breakdown of the change in profit, management could decide whether or not attention was needed to increase sales volume or reduce manufacturing costs in the future.

The same analysis could be performed using full, rather than variable, costing. In this case changes in factory overhead costs will be included in the variance summary, since the analysis will not be limited to direct costs, as in the previous case. The variance summary will differ from the one calculated above in two respects:

1. The manufacturing cost variance will include the overhead spending variance and the overhead efficiency variance, calculated in the same way we illustrated in Chapter 7.

2. The overhead volume variance will be shown as a separate variance on the variance summary, so that management may be informed as to how such a departure from the planned production volume will affect overall profits.

The following information refers to the Faulkner Corporation for the month of January. Faulkner uses a full costing system and budgets fixed costs at $120,000 at a normal production volume of 200,000 units. (Recall that normal volume is a long run average for the firm.) Using its standard costing system, the firm budgets its gross margin as follows:

	($)	($)
Selling price		10.00
Product cost:		
Variable cost per unit	6.00	
Fixed cost per unit	0.60	
Total cost per unit		6.60
Gross margin		3.40

The firm's actual and budgeted results for the month of July are as follows:

	Actual	Budgeted	Variance
Units sold	12,000	10,000	2,000
Units produced	8,000	10,000	(2,000)
Sales revenue	$118,800	$100,000	$18,000
Standard cost of goods sold	79,200	66,000	(13,200)
Gross margin	38,800	34,000	4,800
Factory cost variances	(5,200)	–	(5,200)
Income	$33,600	$34,000	$(400)

The total variance was $400 unfavorable, which is relatively insignificant given the budgeted profit of $34,000. However, since the firm sold 2,000 more units than it had planned, the unfavorable variance is surprising. A breakdown of the total variance into its various components will provide management with the necessary information to determine why the additional sales volume did not result in larger profits for the period. The following variances will be calculated:

1. Sales volume variance.
2. Production volume variance.
3. Sales price variance.
4. Manufacturing cost variance.

The sales volume variance is derived from the difference between budgeted sales at standard prices and actual sales at standard prices, in both cases using the standard cost of goods sold.

	Budgeted sales, Budgeted prices, Standard cost of goods sold	Actual sales, Budgeted prices, Standard cost of goods sold
Revenue	$100,000	$120,000
CGS	(66,000)	(79,200)
Gross margin	$34,000	$40,800
	$6,800 sales volume variance favorable	

As expected, the volume variance is favorable, and significantly so. Next, the effect of the manufacturing volume variance will be calculated, showing how much the reduction in production volume affects the overall profits. Under- or over-absorbed factory overhead will directly affect net income, since it will be expensed directly on the income statement in the period in which it occurs.

	Actual sales, Budgeted production, Standard cost of goods sold	Actual sales, Actual production, Standard cost of goods sold
Revenue	$120,000	$120,000
CGS	(79,200)	(79,200)
Gross margin	$40,800	$40,800
Under-absorbed overhead	–	(1,200)
Income	$40,800	$39,600
	$1,200 unfavorable production volume variance	

Production volume variance could also be calculated by multiplying the fixed overhead cost per unit, $0.60, times the difference between budgeted production volume, 10,000 units, and actual production volume, 8,000 units. It is exactly the same variance as the overhead volume variance introduced in Chapter 6, and represents the amount of the fixed manufacturing cost not accounted for in the cost of goods sold for the period.

The sales price variance can be calculated next, and simply represents the change in net income due to a change in selling price from the budgeted price. Often this is due to volume discounts or price reductions to get rid of large inventories.

	Actual sales, Budgeted prices, Budgeted cost of goods sold, Actual production	Actual sales, Actual prices, Budgeted cost of goods sold, Actual production
Revenue	$120,000	$118,800
CGS	(79,200)	(79,200)
Gross margin	$40,800	$39,600
Underabsorbed overhead	(1,200)	(1,200)
Income	$39,600	$38,400
	$1,200 sales price variance unfavorable	

The sales price variance can also be found by simply comparing the first line of the chart above, actual sales at actual prices, and actual sales at budgeted prices. The rest of the information is shown in order to demonstrate that all other figures are being held constant to isolate the effect of the price variance. The last variance to be found is the manufacturing cost variance, which is really the sum of the direct materials and direct labor variances. As noted above, only a summary figure will be given in a report sent to top management, unless unusual circumstances require them to give attention to the details of the price and quantity variances.

	Actual sales, Actual prices, Standard cost of goods sold, Actual production	Actual sales, Actual prices, Actual cost of goods sold, Actual production
Revenue	$118,000	$118,000
CGS	(79,200)	(83,200)
Gross margin	$38,800	$34,800
Underabsorbed overhead	(1,200)	(1,200)
Income	$37,600	$33,600
	$4,000 manufacturing cost variance unfavorable	

Now the total profit variance can be explained by reference to its different components. As may be seen from the chart of variances, the total variance is due mainly to two effects: the sales volume was considerably higher than anticipated, and the direct manufacturing costs were higher than budgeted. Because these two variances canceled each other out, the total profit variance was not large. But the details of the performance analysis should alert management to some areas where problems may exist in the future.

Sales volume variance	$6,800	Favorable
Production volume variance	$1,200	Unfavorable
Sales price variance	$1,200	Unfavorable
Manufacturing cost variance	$4,000	Unfavorable

SALES MIX VARIANCE

When a firm sells more than one product another source of profit variance is the sales mix, or the ratio of one product to another sold. Since the gross margin on the product types may not be identical, an increase in the volume of one sold to another could change the overall profits even if the total revenues of the firm were the same. Thus management is often interested in knowing the effect of the sales mix, and it is calculated separately from the sales volume variance. Computation of the sales mix variance will be illustrated with the following example.

Suppose a hotel offers two types of room rates, the regular daily rate and the special rate. The special rate is accompanied by a slight reduction in services, so that the cost of services associated with it is slightly lower. The budgeted rates and service costs for the two product types are:

	Daily ($)	Special ($)
Room rate	120	80
Cost of services	60	55
Gross margin	60	25

The hotel expects a room occupancy of 300 days a year, and plans to sell a room at the daily rate 80% of the time, and at the special rate 20% of the time. Thus the budgeted gross margin per room per year is:

	Daily ($)	Special ($)	Total ($)
Room charges	28,800	4,800	33,600
Cost of services	14,400	3,300	17,700
Gross margin	14,400	1,500	15,900

The actual sales data for the year indicated that the rooms were sold in a ratio of 70 to 30, and that the total sales volume was down. The data is recorded as follows:

	Daily ($)	Special ($)	Total ($)
Room charges	23,520	6,720	30,240
Cost of services	11,760	4,620	16,380
Gross margin	11,760	2,100	13,860

The difference between the actual gross margin of $13,860 and the budgeted gross margin of $15,900 is partly due to the reduction in overall occupancy and partly due to a change in the sales mix. Applying the variance analysis to the hotel data, we can break down the total variance into its two components as follows: Actual mix and budgeted mix both refer to the cost of goods sold, in the first case calculated as the standard cost of services at the actual 70/30 sales mix; in the second case the standard cost of services is calculated at the planned mix of 80/20.

	Actual sales actual mix ($)	Actual sales budgeted mix ($)
Revenues	30,240	30,240
Cost of services	16,380	15,390
Gross margin	13,860	14,850
$990 sales mix variance unfavorable		

The sales mix variance is $990, and represents the amount of the total variance which is due to sales mix alone. In other words, if the hotel had maintained an occupancy rate of 300 days a year, as budgeted, but had sold the rooms in a 70/30 proportion, the reduction in profits would have been about $1,000 per room.

The sales volume variance, net of the mix variance, can now be calculated.

	Actual sales budgeted mix ($)	Budgeted sales budgeted mix ($)
Revenues	30,240	33,600
Cost of services	15,390	17,700
Gross margin	14,850	15,900
$1,050 sales volume variance unfavorable		

The portion of the total variance attributable to the reduction in occupancy rates is $1,050 per room. Breaking down the total variance in this way allows management to determine the gravity of each of the departures from the budget, and to focus its attention where it believes the payoff will be the highest.

SUMMARY

In this chapter a few of the ways in which management may break down the information contained in a profit summary

have been illustrated. Many other variances may be calculated from the actual and budgeted results for a period, and
the number routinely analyzed depends on the attention
management feels it can profitably give to performance
details. This will differ from firm to firm; however, the basic
techniques remain constant across most variance reports.

Chapter 11

The Role of Financial Accounts

The purpose of this chapter and that following is to introduce the student to the fundamentals of financial accounting. Whereas management accounting is concerned with the preparation and analysis of financial information for decision-making purposes within the firm, financial accounting focuses on the presentation of financial information to users outside of the firm. Such users include stockholders, creditors, financial analysts, employees, and government organizations, with the exception of the taxing authority. (The latter requires that financial information be prepared according to specific rules established by it.)

All users require information on the profitability and associated returns on the firm's assets on the current financial position or wealth of the firm, and on the liquidity of the firm and its ability to pay debts. Undoubtedly all users would like knowledge of the future returns of the firm and the associated risks of investment. Forecasts of such information are rarely released by firms, however, and each user is forced to make his own assessment of the future on the basis of the past information published by the firm.

Firms registered with the Securities and Exchange Commission (SEC), which includes those traded on any of the organized stock markets, are required to prepare and submit to the SEC and to their stockholders annual financial statements as well as certain quarterly information. The purpose of this regulation is to ensure that stockholders have access to the necessary data to determine whether or not management is fulfilling its stewardship function with respect to their investment. Many people believe that the great stock market crash of 1929 was in part due to the fact that firms were not required to submit any information to their stockholders, and therefore could misrepresent the firm's economic potential. Irrespective of the validity of this conclusion, it was because of the 1929 debacle that the SEC was established as an oversight board for publicly owned firms and those firms required to submit financial information to their public owners. If, on the basis of the firm's published results, the stockholders are not satisfied with the performance of management, their voting rights give them the power to fire the firm's managers and to select new ones to oversee the firm.

The Financial Accounting Standards Board (FASB) determines the rules governing the preparation of financial information for all publicly owned firms. That is, it determines what measurement rules are to be applied when a firm is representing the results of its activities during the previous year, or its current financial position. These rules are collectively known as "generally accepted accounting principles," or GAAP. The FASB's authority is derived from the recognition given its pronouncements by the Securities and Exchange Commission, which in turn derives its authority from the Congress.

In order to insure that the information prepared by the management of the firm fairly represents its financial condition, the SEC also requires that the information be audited by an independent auditor. The auditor's investigation of the veracity of the firm's financial statements includes an analysis of its internal control systems as well as confirmation of the physical quantities reported by the firm. Upon completion of the audit the auditor certifies that the statements present fairly the financial position of XYZ firm at December 31, and the results of their operations and the changes in their financial position for the year then ended, and in conformity with generally accepted accounting principles applied on a consistent basis.

The three basic statements prepared by firms are the balance sheet, the income statement, and the statement of changes in financial position. The income statement represents the economic results of the firm's operations over the previous year. Since the information is derived from historical data, it cannot be directly translated to yield predictions for the future; however, with thoughtful analysis of income statement and other data, an investor could make a reasonable estimate of the future profitability of the firm.

The balance sheet provides a statement of the firm's total assets, liabilities, and owners' equity (which includes stock ownership and earnings retained by the firm) as of the close of the fiscal year. These amounts are stated at their historical costs, which means that a user of the information might want to make some adjustments to take into account the effects of inflation, particularly on the various assets. In recent years the FASB has required firms to restate some of their reported financial information to allow for inflation, thereby easing the burden on the individual investor.

The third required statement, the statement of changes in financial position, shows the flow of resources through the firm during the year; that is, where did they get their funds and what did they do with them? Each of these statements will be reviewed in turn.

THE BALANCE SHEET

The balance sheet may be thought of as a financial position statement or a statement of wealth. The three kinds of accounts to be found on a balance sheet are the assets, the liabilities, and the owner's equity accounts. The balance sheet represents the fundamental accounting equation:

$$\text{Assets} = \text{Liabilities} + \text{Owner's equity}$$

This equation illustrates the function of the balance sheet: to show at any given time the wealth held by the firm, and its methods of obtaining that wealth. If a firm had no owner's equity, it would mean that it had borrowed the money to purchase everything which it currently owned; similarly, if a firm had no liabilities, then this would indicate that all its assets were purchased with funds originally invested by the owners, or with profits made and reinvested by the firm.

Assets

An asset may be defined as something which has been acquired by the firm at some positive cost, and which is expected to bring economic benefit to the firm in the future. This definition means that certain things belonging to a firm which are of obviously great value, for example the recipe for Coca-Cola, will not be listed on the balance sheet since they were not purchased by the firm. Similarly, assets may appreciate well beyond their value as recorded on the balance sheet without this fact being reconized in the accounts. Thus the numbers recorded on the balance sheet as the "value" of the firm's assets must be interpreted cautiously. One obvious reminder of this shortcoming of financial accounting is that the prices of most firms which trade publicly on one of the organized stock markets are significantly higher than their "book values," or their value as recorded by the accounting system.

Assets are grouped under two headings: current assets and non-current, or fixed, assets. The former are those assets which the firm expects to consume in its earnings process within one operating cycle, or more commonly within one year. Ordinarily, current assets will encompass the following set of accounts:

1. Cash: Firms will usually hold a certain amount of cash in checking or short-term savings accounts to meet their normal operating expenses. The amount of cash required will obviously vary from industry to industry, and even from firm to firm. Money held in checking accounts is included as cash.

2. Accounts Receivable: A firm which sells goods on credit will set up an account to keep track of the amounts owed it by its customers. Since the use of credit invariably means that the firm will incur losses from customers who are unable or unwilling to satisfy their obligations, Accounts Receivable will usually be accompanied by a **contra-account**, Allowance for Doubtful Accounts. In this account management will record its best estimate of the amount it expects to lose on its outstanding receivables at any given time. One of the responsibilities of the firm's independent auditors in its yearly review is to determine whether or not management has made sufficient allowance for losses when stating the value of its receivables.

3. Inventory: One or more inventory accounts will be listed among the current assets of most firms, representing goods held for immediate sale or raw materials being converted into finished goods. These goods are recorded at their acquisition, or historical, cost. Since fluctuations in prices (either inflationary or simply due to changes in the supply and demand functions which govern prices) will cause the unit cost of a firm's inventory to vary over time, certain conventions have been established for keeping track of the cost of goods currently held and those recorded as expenses on the income statement. The details of these cost conventions need not concern us here other than to describe their effects on the balance sheet values. A firm may cost its inventory using either FIFO (first-in, first-out) or LIFO (last-in, first-out) as its cost flow assumption. FIFO will mean that as the firm acquires inventory, the costs associated with those purchased earliest will be recorded on the income statement as the cost of the goods sold in the period. If inflation is a serious factor affecting inventory costs, then the effect will be that the lower costs are reported on the income statement, and the more recent and therefore higher costs reported on the balance sheet. Under LIFO, the effects will be reversed: The costs reported on the income statement will reflect more recent, higher prices, while those on the balance sheet will be those associated with an earlier period, and therefore lower. Neither FIFO nor LIFO is an inherently superior costing method; each requires the investor or analyst to carefully interpret the relative costs reported on the income statement and balance sheet. It is, however, far more common for American firms to use LIFO since the IRS requires firms which use it for tax purposes to use it for financial reporting purposes too. Most firms benefit from lower taxes when they report costs on a LIFO basis. Regardless of whether LIFO or FIFO is adopted, if the market value of the firm's inventory is below the historical cost, the firm must "write down" the inventory to market and record a loss on the income statement for the period.

4. Prepaid items: If rent, insurance, taxes or other similar items are paid before the period in which they are due, they are recorded as assets on the firm's books. These represent potential benefits which will accrue to the firm as the assets expire. As the firm receives the benefits, that is, occupies the rented building, or is covered by the insurance policy for a period, these assets are expensed onto the income statement.

5. Marketable securities: Sometimes a firm holds investments in the securities of other firms with the intention of liquidating them and using the proceeds for some other purpose in the near future. In this case these securities are listed as current assets and valued at the lower of their historical cost or their market value as of the last day of the fiscal year. The lower of cost or market convention prevents the value of these assets from being overstated on the balance sheet.

In addition to its current assets, a firm will list on its balance sheet non-current, or fixed, assets. These are long-term investments in assets which the firm uses to generate earnings. Among those most commonly found in the financial statements are the following:

1. Property, plant and equipment: This includes office buildings, factories, and machinery owned by the firm. Each capital item will have a depreciation account associated with it, in which will be recorded the amount of the asset which is assumed to have "expired" each year. The amount of depreciation recorded each year is not determined by physical inspection, but rather by an arbitrary accounting rule applied to the asset's historical cost. The most commonly used depreciation method is **straight-line**, which means that the asset's cost is depreciated in equal amounts over its estimated useful life. For example, if a machine was expected to last for 10 years, then one-tenth of its total cost would be recorded as depreciation expense each year, and subtracted from the amount recorded as the asset value on the balance sheet. As the asset is depreciated, a corresponding expense will be recorded on the firm's income statement.

2. Land: Land is recorded at its historical cost, and is not subject to depreciation. However, neither is it subject to appreciation, which means that the value of land on a firm's books will in most cases understate its true value. In general, the more recently the land was acquired, the closer will be its book value to its market value.

3. Leased property: Some firms, for example many airline companies, do not own their own equipment but rather lease these items on a long-term basis from a supplier or manufacturer. Several years ago the FASB decided that many of these leases were more like financing arrangements than true leases and should be treated as such for accounting purposes. (Imagine if you rented an apartment on a non-cancelable thirty-year lease which required you to make yearly payments including a charge for interest, and gave you an option to buy the apartment at a nominal price at the end of the thirty years; is this more like a lease or a mortgage?) Leases which satisfy certain criteria set up by the FASB are classified as "capital leases" and must be treated by the lessee as an asset and an accompanying liability. When a leasehold is listed among a firm's assets, it will always be accompanied by a long-term liability, representing the present value of the required payments under the lease.

4. Investment in non-consolidated subsidiary: If a firm owns a substantial amount of the stock of another firm, but less than half, it will list its ownership rights as an asset. The accounting rules for investments in other firms is a complicated issue, and far beyond the scope of this review.

5. Intangibles: When a firm purchases another firm outright, the amount it pays for it will frequently exceed the fair market value of the firm's physical assets. This is because the value of a company does not reside entirely in the things it owns but also in its reputation, its operating expertise, its connections with suppliers or distributors, etc. The amount by which a purchase price exceeds the fair market value of the assets is referred to as "goodwill," and is listed on the purchasing firm's balance sheet as an asset. The useful life of this intangible asset is arbitrarily determined to be less than or equal to forty years (the firm may decide to use any number of years less than forty under GAAP) and the value of the goodwill is amortized (amortization is simply depreciation applied to an intangible asset) over that period. A firm may also purchase a patent or a trademark and create an intangible asset, which is then amortized in the same way as goodwill.

Just as a firm classifies its assets as current and non-current, it will also separate **its liabilities** into current liabilities and long-term liabilities. Among current liabilities are typically listed the following accounts:

1. Accounts Payable: This is analogous to the current asset, Accounts Receivable. When a firm purchases goods (inventories or services) on credit, it must record its obligation to pay as a liability. Since few trade creditors extend credit for periods as long as a year, most of these payables are listed as current.

2. Salaries Payable: When an employee performs services for a company, the wages paid to him are listed on the income statement as an expense. If the employee is not paid immediately, then the firm must also record its liability to pay the employee in the future.

3. Taxes Payable: This represents money which must be paid to the IRS or a local taxing authority within the current year.

4. Dividends Payable: Most firms declare regular quarterly dividends to their stockholders as a return on the stockholder's investment. When dividends have been declared but the checks have not yet been sent to the stockholders, then a payable is set up on the firm's books.

5. Notes Payable, or Current Portion of Long-Term Debt Payable: Frequently a firm will finance part of its activities with a short-term loan from a bank. This may be referred to as a note payable, and is recorded among the liabilities. When a firm borrows money on a long-term basis, the contract sometimes calls for payment of part of the debt at an earlier date than the remainder. Whenever part of the loan must be repaid within the current year, the obligation is listed among the current liabilities.

Among the non-current liabilities of the firm, there are three common entries:

1. Bonds Payable: Long-term debt is usually issued in the form of a bond, on which is made regular interest payments and a lump-sum payment of the principal at the end of a certain number of years. The obligation to pay the principal is recorded as a non-current liability on the firm's books.

2. Present value of leasehold obligation: Recall that a firm might have listed among its non-current assets leased property or equipment. When this is the case, the firm must list the corresponding liability. The amount which is recorded is the present value of the total amount to be paid over the life of the lease.

3. Deferred taxes: Because the IRS has its own set of rules governing the reporting of a firm's income, the taxes a firm is required to pay will not always equal the tax expense it reports to its stockholders. For example, suppose a firm is subject to a 50% tax on net income. It will calculate net income according to GAAP to report to its stockholders, and record tax expense as 50% of that amount. However, when it actually prepares its tax return to the IRS, net income must be calculated in terms of the IRS accounting rules, not GAAP. Consequently, net income may be different, and the actual amount of a firm's tax payment will therefore be different. When the tax paid to the IRS is less than the tax expense shown to the stockholders (this situation is more usually observed than the reverse) the difference is shown as a liability to pay taxes in the future (but not within the current year), and referred to as Deferred Taxes.

The Owner's Equity accounts include the capital stock accounts and the retained earnings accounts.

1. Common stock: The common stock accounts represent the amount of money paid by the firm's owners for a right to share in the future dividends declared by the firm. Two common stock accounts will be listed on the financial statements: Common Stock at Par, and Additional Paid-In Capital. The distinction between these two accounts is of little interest for most purposes; the par value of stock is a legal definition and has no intrinsic economic meaning. If a firm issued stock at $25 per share, typically the par value would be a small percentage of that amount, say $1. In this case, for each share that was purchased, $1 would be listed in the Common Stock at Par account, and $24 in the Additional Paid-In Capital account. Note that future exchanges of stock between private individuals do not affect the amounts listed in these accounts. Amounts listed in the accounts reflect only initial sale of stock transactions.

2. Preferred stock: Preferred stock represents another category of ownership rights that are handled in all respects like the common stock accounts discussed above. The distinction between common and preferred stocks has to do with the certainty associated with dividends payment. When preferred stocks are issued, the dividend to be paid is specified and remains constant in the future. The return on preferred stocks is typically lower than on common stocks due to the lesser associated risk.

3. Retained earnings: Retained earnings accounts represent the portion of net income that is not paid out to stockholders in the form of dividends. Retained earnings therefore represents that portion of income that has been reinvested in the firm. It is important to note that retained earnings is not synonymous with cash retained by the firm. Since net income is not equal to cash, neither can retained earnings be equated with cash.

THE INCOME STATEMENT

The income statement is a summary of the change in wealth of the firm during the previous accounting period resulting from the firm's operations or other activities (for example, the disposal of a portion of the firm's fixed assets). The entries on the income statement consist of revenues, representing increases in the firm's wealth, and expenses, representing decreases in the firm's wealth. Obviously when revenues exceed expenses the firm realizes a profit for the period; when expenses exceed revenues the firm incurs a loss.

Since all revenue and expense items are not synonymous with cash receipts and disbursements, the net income figure will not represent a corresponding increase in cash for the firm. Accounting seeks to measure changes in wealth of the firm, not simply changes in the cash balance. Therefore an increase in accounts receivable is treated as an increase in wealth, and the depreciation on plant and equipment is treated as a decrease in wealth, even though neither of these has an immediate effect on the firm's cash position. Formally, this accounting concept is referred to as accrual accounting.

Although measuring income as the change in wealth from all sources provides the financial statement user with important information, it does leave unanswered some important questions about the firm's ability to pay its debts or meet its other cash needs in the future. An investor, and in particular a creditor, would want information about how the firm is actually financing its current operations, and how quickly the firm can generate cash to meet its immediate needs. Some of these questions can be answered with the use of ratio analysis, the topic of the next chapter; others can be answered with the help of the information contained in the Statement of Changes in Financial Position.

THE STATEMENT OF CHANGES IN FINANCIAL POSITION

The Statement of Changes in Financial Position is also known informally by a number of other names: the funds flow statement, the working capital statement, the sources and applications of funds statement, or the "where got, where gone" statement. The latter is the most accurate description of the statement's purpose; it explains where the firm got its funds and what it did with them during the year.

The statement is not difficult to understand or interpret once the definition of funds has been grasped. A funds flow statement could be prepared using cash as the definition of funds; then the statement would show where the firm got its cash during the year, and what it did with it. However, the FASB does not require this level of detail about the firm's cash position. Instead, firms may define funds as working capital, or current assets minus current liabilities.

The balances in the firm's current asset and current liabilities accounts represent the results of its manufacturing and selling operations at any given time. Inventory is quickly converted to accounts receivable through the sales process, accounts receivable converted to cash upon collection, and cash used to pay creditors, thereby reducing accounts payable. Working capital provides a quick summary of these activities: do current assets exceed current liabilities, or vice versa?

Changes in working capital are considered important because working capital provides a rough measure of the firm's liquidity. Current assets are those assets which will be used to generate income during the year, and current liabilities are those liabilities which must be paid off during the year. If current liabilities greatly exceed the current assets of the firm, or more importantly, if the relationship between current assets and current liabilities changes dramatically, it may be a signal that the firm is having some problems meeting its obligations. Obviously a cash flow statement would provide this information more directly, but a working capital statement, or funds flow statement, provides a first approximation of it, and in many cases is a sufficient source of information for a user. Furthermore, a working capital statement can be converted to a cash flow statement by examining changes in the individual current asset and current liability accounts.

Obviously the only purpose of a funds flow statement cannot be to show the changes in working capital during the year, because this would be more easily accomplished by a simple comparison of the balance sheet at two dates. The change in working capital is a summary of the changes in the firm's current accounts on two successive dates. The statement also provides detail about the changes in the firm's non-current assets and non-current liabilities and owner's equity during the year. A financial statement user could examine two successive balance sheets and draw some inferences about the firm's activities during the year; for example, that it purchased new equipment, or issued additional long-term debt, or sold common stock. The funds flow statement makes explicit this information.

The basic relationships shown on a working capital statement are those described in Figure 22. The sources of funds

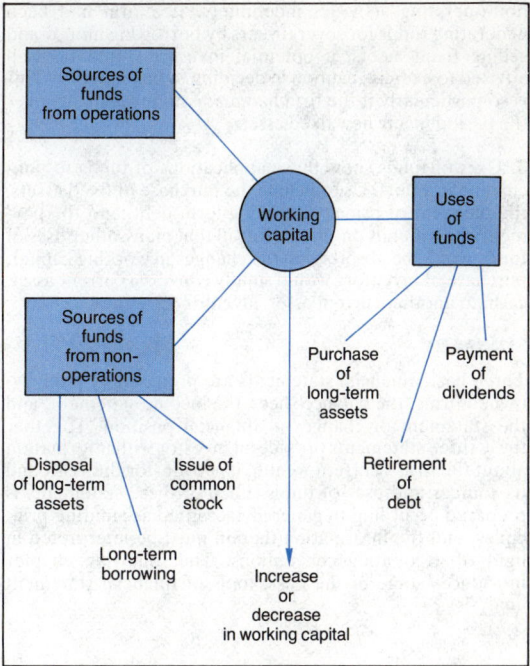

Figure 22. Sources and uses of funds

are divided into those from operations and those from non-operations. The total sources of funds do not necessarily equal the total uses of funds during any year. If working capital increased, then the total sources of funds exceeded the total uses. If working capital decreased, then the total uses of funds exceeded the sources.

1. Funds from operations include any of the firm's normal profit-making activities which increase working capital, less those which decrease working capital. Usually this may be approximated by the net income figure if depreciation expense is added back. Depreciation is added back because it is an expense which does not reduce current assets (no cash is paid out) nor increase current liabilities (no payable is created), and therefore has no effect on working capital. Several other items in the income statement have the same characteristic, and will be treated similarly, but this level of detail is beyond the scope of this discussion.

2. Funds from non-operating activities include the sale of fixed assets, the issuing of long-term debt, and the sale of common stock. All of these will provide the firm with cash for the period, and therefore increase working capital. The reason they are shown separately from the funds from oper-ations is that a firm cannot continue to generate funds from non-operating activities indefinitely. If a firm had been generating funds for several years by borrowing money and selling fixed assets, a potential investor would be well advised to exercise caution in deciding to buy its stock. This is so particularly if the firm had made no investments over the period in any new fixed assets.

3. Uses of funds show those applications of funds to non-current accounts. Uses include the purchase of fixed assets, the payment of principal on long-term debt, and the payment of dividends on stock. (Recall that many other uses of funds would be absorbed in the changes in working capital; purchase of inventory would simply convert a current asset, cash, to another current asset, inventory.)

SUMMARY

Three basic financial statements are prepared by publicly-owned firms: the balance sheet, the income statement, and the statement of changes in financial position. Together these three statements provide an investor with information about the firm's current wealth, its profits for the year, and its sources and uses of funds. Each of these statements is prepared according to generally accepted accounting principles, and the information therein must be interpreted in light of accounting conventions. The following chapter introduces some of the basic tools of financial statement analysis.

Chapter 12

Financial Statement Analysis

Financial statement users are interested in evaluating a firm's economic performance in order to make some decisions concerning investment or disinvestment. However, the information contained in the firm's three basic financial statements, the balance sheet, the income statement, and the statement of changes in financial position, does not provide an investor or financial analyst with sufficient information to draw any real conclusions about the firm's performance. For example, the statements might show that the firm earned $5 million, and had assets valued at $100 million. Does this represent a good performance for the year or not, and could this firm be expected to continue to perform at the same level in the future? There is no way to answer these questions without comparing the firm's performance this year to its performance in previous years, and/or the performance of other firms in the same industry. This is the purpose of the techniques introduced in this chapter, to provide some common bases of comparison so that any firm's financial statement may be evaluated against a standard.

Two methods are commonly used for comparing financial results across time and across firms: the first is common size statements, and the second ratio analysis. Of course, to gain a full understanding of a firm and its economic prospects, many other sources of information are needed besides financial statements; knowledge of the markets for the firm's products, developments in the industry's technology and forecasts of macroeconomics variables such as interest rates all provide useful information to a financial analyst. In addition, some analysts have developed valuation models, which incorporate past and current financial information into a regression model for the purpose of forecasting future performance. None of these more sophisticated methods will be discussed here; interested readers should consult the textbooks on the subject of financial statement analysis listed at the back of this book.

COMMON SIZE STATEMENTS

One standard of comparison for a firm's financial position is provided by other firms in the same industry. However, when firms differ radically in size, comparing the financial statements directly will lead to ambiguous or misleading conclusions. One way to control for size differences is to scale down all the numbers so that they are represented as percentages rather than actual values. In other words, a firm's accounts receivable will be expressed not as a dollar figure, but rather as a percentage of total assets. These may be compared with the industry averages in order to determine the relative performance of two firms.

INFORMATION NEEDS AND FINANCIAL RATIOS

Financial ratios are calculated to provide answers to certain questions investors might have about the firm. Many different financial ratios have been proposed in the literature, some of which are more commonly used than others. These ratios may be grouped into four categories, according to their basic purpose:

1. Tests of profitability.
2. Tests of liquidity.
3. Tests of capital structure or leverage.
4. Turnover ratios.
5. Common Stock and Market Value Ratios.

Analysts and practitioners classify these in various ways; these differences are of little concern to us. Understanding the purpose of individual ratios and the means of calculating them is the primary focus of this chapter.

TESTS OF PROFITABILITY

Since it is the ultimate objective of a firm to generate profits, it is of obvious interest to investors to assess the relative ability of the firm to do so. A number of different measures of profitability exist, all of which compare some measure of earnings to an investment base.

1. Return on total assets

$$\frac{\text{Net income after taxes}+\text{Interest expense}-(\text{Tax rate}\times\text{Interest expense})}{\text{Total assets}}$$

The return on total assets indicates how successfully the firm is using its total asset base to generate earnings. The reason that interest expense, minus the tax benefit of interest, is added to net income in the numerator is that part of the firm's earning capacity is dedicated to repaying interest on debt. Since assets financed by debt are included in the denominator, the earnings used in repaying debt obligations need to be included in the numerator. The denominator is usually calculated as the average total assets during the year, or beginning balance in total assets plus ending balance in total assets divided by 2. The average is used because the ratio seeks to identify what the firm did with the resources available to it: using the beginning balance in total assets would understate the assets the firm had during the year, and using the ending balance would overstate the assets available.

2. Return on Shareholders' equity

$$\frac{\text{Net income minus preferred dividends}}{\text{Common shareholders' equity}}$$

This ratio measures the efficiency with which the firm is

using assets financed by common stock to generate earnings for the common stockholders. Preferred dividends are subtracted because earnings paid out to preferred stockholders in the form of dividends are not available to common stockholders. As is the case with the previous ratio, the denominator is the average shareholders' equity during the year.

3. Operating Profit Ratio

$$\frac{\text{Sales} - \text{Cost of goods sold} - \text{Selling and administrative expenses}}{\text{Sales}}$$

This ratio shows how much of each dollar of revenue the firm generates is available for purposes other than paying the firm's normal operating expenses. Other uses of the operating profit include payment of interest on debt, payment of dividends, and capital investment. Obviously the smaller the operating profit, the less flexibility the firm will have in its dividend or investment policy.

LIQUIDITY

A firm's liquidity is usually defined as its ability to meet its short-term financial obligations as they come due. Liquidity is, therefore, the firm's cash-generating capacity in comparison to its short-term needs, and is of particular interest to short-term creditors. Several ratios are used by analysts to assess liquidity.

1. Current ratio

$$\frac{\text{Current assets}}{\text{Current liabilities}}$$

This is the ratio of a firm's liquid assets to its immediate financial obligations. The numerator consists usually of cash, accounts receivable, inventories, pre-paid expenses, and marketable securities (if the latter are classified as current assets). The denominator is the sum of all short-term payables.

2. Quick ratio

$$\frac{\text{Quick assets}}{\text{Current liabilities}}$$

Objections have been raised as to the usefulness of the current ratio in testing a firm's liquidity, since such current assets as inventories and pre-paid expenses may not convert readily to cash. This reservation is particularly important in the case of troubled firms. The quick ratio uses only assets which could be used to pay off debts on short notice: these include cash, accounts receivable, and short-term marketable securities. The denominator incorporates all current liabilities.

3. Defensive interval

$$\frac{\text{Defensive assets}}{\text{Average daily operating expenditures}}$$

Both the current ratio and the quick ratio are **stock** measures, or static measures, as opposed to flow measures. The firm's ability to pay its debts as they come due really depends on the amounts and timings of future cash flows, not the amounts of current assets and current liabilities at a single point in time. A ratio used to measure liquidity as a flow concept is the defensive interval. Defensive assets are equivalent to quick assets. The denominator is an estimate of the daily operating expenses requiring cash outlays. The ratio yields a figure representing the number of days a firm could continue to operate using its current liquid assets to pay operating expenses.

TURNOVER RATIOS

In addition to the profitability measures listed above, the firm's efficiency in using its asset base may be examined by means of turnover ratios. They provide indices of the velocity with which various items are moved through the firm: inventory turnover and accounts receivable turnover; or to show the efficiency with which the firm uses its asset base to generate sales or profits.

1. Inventory turnover

$$\frac{\text{Sales or cost of goods sold}}{\text{Average inventory}}$$

An increase in the size of inventory on the balance sheet may indicate an increase in the necessary amount of inventory held due to an increase in sales volume (that is, a planned increase in inventory), or an increase in inventory held due to an unexpected decrease in sales volume. These two possibilities may be distinguished with the use of the inventory turnover, which will indicate how many times the (average) amount of inventory on the balance sheet was replaced during the year.

2. Accounts receivable turnover

$$\frac{\text{Sales}}{\text{Average (net) accounts receivable}}$$

Accumulating a large balance in accounts receivable without collecting any money from customer sales suggests a firm might be having some problems consummating its transactions. If the accounts receivable turnover decreases significantly from one year to the next, this is a warning signal that the firm might have some liquidity problems in the immediate future, and risk bankruptcy if the situation worsened.

3. Total assets turnover

$$\frac{\text{Sales}}{\text{Total assets}}$$

This ratio measures a firm's ability to generate sales from a given asset base. Since a high volume of sales does not necessarily mean that the firm is earning large profits, this ratio is often accompanied by an index of a firm's operating profit as a percentage of sales. High margins (operating profits to sales) tend to be associated with low asset turnover, and vice versa. The supermarket industry provides a good example; it is characterized by a very low return per dollar of sales, and high volume of sales.

CAPITAL STRUCTURE RATIOS

Capital structure ratios provide information on the firm's long-term debt obligations and the associated risk. Since fixed interest payments must be met before the firm may pay dividends, a firm which is highly leveraged (that is, finances a large portion of its assets with debt as opposed to equity capital) appears to have higher risk from the point of view of its stockholders.

1. Long-term debt to equity

$$\frac{\text{Long-term debt}}{\text{Stockholders' equity}}$$

In principle this ratio is simple to understand, but many difficulties are encountered in actually defining the components of debt to be included in the numerator. Many firms issue convertible securities, which are hybrids of debt and equity, and the placement of these will obviously affect the value of the ratio. Also, the question of whether or not to include deferred taxes as debt has not resulted in a consensus among financial analysts.

2. Total debt to equity

$$\frac{\text{Total debt}}{\text{Shareholders' equity}}$$

This ratio is the same as the one above except that current liabilities are included in the numerator as debt. It obviously suffers from the same definitional problems as the previous ratio. In addition, both ratios may be calculated using either the book value (the amount written on the financial statements) or the market value (the price at which the listed bonds are currently trading) as the numerator. Book value is more frequently used, since it is the easier number to find.

3. Times interest earned

$$\frac{\text{Operating income}}{\text{Required annual interest payments}}$$

This ratio provides a direct measure of the firm's current safety margin with respect to its long-term debt obligations. It represents the number of times the firm's current operating income covers its interest payments.

COMMON STOCK AND MARKET VALUE RATIOS

1. Earnings per share

$$\frac{\text{Net income available to common stockholders}}{\text{Number of common shares outstanding}}$$

This ratio indicates how much income is available to each stockholder for distribution in the form of dividends. Comparisons of earnings per share across firms tend not to be very meaningful, since it is entirely dependent on the number of shares a firm has issued, a decision which is entirely arbitrary.

2. Book value per share

$$\frac{\text{Total shareholders' equity}}{\text{Number of common shares outstanding}}$$

The book value per share is often compared to the market value per share of stock to determine if the firm is currently "undervalued" or "overvalued." The validity of this comparison is much disputed by market analysts, but the ratio is one of the most commonly quoted concerning a firm's value.

3. Price/earnings ratio

$$\frac{\text{Market price per share}}{\text{Earnings per share}}$$

The price/earnings ratio is probably the most commonly cited index of a firm's performance. The price at which the firm is currently trading is viewed by many as the best possible estimate of its future performance, one which incorporates all available information about its expected return and the associated risk.

SUMMARY

The discussion above has introduced some of the most important commonly used ratios in financial statement analysis. Familiarity with a firm and its industry will allow an analyst to draw more insights from examination of a particular set of ratios. In addition, a complete understanding of accounting conventions will allow a financial statement user to interpret the information contained in a set of ratios, and prevent the drawing of misleading conclusions.

Further Reading

Anthony, R.N. and Dearden, J., *Management Control Systems: Cases and Headings* (Irwin, Fourth Edition, 1980)

Anthony, R.N. and Welsch, G.A., *Fundamentals of Management Accounting* (Irwin, 1977)

Bierman, H. and Smidt, S., *The Capital Budgeting Decision* (Macmillan, Fifth Edition, 1980)

Foster, G., *Financial Statement Analysis* (Prentice-Hall, 1978)

Hopwood, A., *Accounting and Human Behavior* (Prentice-Hall, 1976)

Horngren, C.T., *Cost Accounting: A Managerial Emphasis* (Prentice-Hall, Fifth Edition, 1982)

Horngren, C.T., *Introduction to Management Accounting* (Prentice-Hall, 1982)

Lev, B., *Financial Statement Analysis: A New Approach* (Prentice-Hall, 1974)

Miller, D.W. and Starr, M.K., *Executive Decisions and Operations Research* (Prentice-Hall, Second Edition, 1969)

Schiff, M. and Lewin, Y., *Behavioral Aspects of Accounting* (Prentice-Hall, 1974)

Shillinglaw, G., *Accounting: A Management Approach* (Irwin, Seventh Edition, 1982)

Shillinglaw, G., *Managerial Cost Accounting* (Irwin, Fourth Edition, 1977)

Summers, E.L., *An Introduction to Accounting for Decision Making and Control* (Irwin, 1974)

Van Horne, J., *Financial Management and Policy* (Prentice-Hall, Fifth Edition, 1980)

Welsch, G., *Budgeting: Profit Planning and Control* (Prentice-Hall, Fourth Edition, 1976)

Glossary

Absorption (of costs) The sharing out of overhead in such a way as to charge such costs to production.

Accounts receivable turnover The ratio of sales to average accounts receivable, an indicator of the firm's efficiency in collecting its receivables as they come due.

Accruals concept The accounting concept which emphasizes that accounts are prepared on the basis of revenues earned and expenses incurred in a period, irrespective of the cash flows occurring.

Allocation (of costs) The charging of costs to the specific cost center by which they were incurred.

Apportionment (of costs) The sharing out, between cost centers, of those overheads which do not relate specifically to one cost center, e.g. power, rent and rates, etc.

Asset turnover The ratio of sales to assets, usually calculated to measure the efficiency of use of assets.

Authoritarian budget A budget which has been imposed by management with little or no consultation with participants.

Balance sheet A statement of Assets, Liabilities, and Owners' Equity.

Batch costing A system of recording costs of production in such a way as to arrive at the cost of a batch or group of production.

Benefit cost ratio This ratio measures the relationship between the present value of inflows and the present value of outflows expected from capital investments. It is commonly used to rank capital projects in situations where there is a shortage of funds.

Break-even analysis The analysis of performance involving the segregation of fixed and variable costs in such a way as to identify the break-even point and the effect of changes in output on overall profitability.

Budget A detailed plan of action for an organization (usually) for the next year, presented in financial terms.

Budgetary control A system of comparing actual results with budgeted figures, highlighting differences between them and ensuring that remedial action is taken quickly.

Capital Those funds contributed by the owners of a firm or attributable to the owner through profitable transactions.

Capital investment appraisal The evaluation of proposals for acquiring new fixed assets so as to choose those projects which will provide the most benefit.

Capital rationing A situation in which there are insufficient funds available to proceed with all capital projects which have a positive net present value. Some form of ranking of projects therefore needs to be devised.

Common size balance sheet A balance sheet in which all items are expressed in percentage terms, so that more effective comparisons can be made among firms.

Confidence level The degree of certainty, or probability, that can be attached to the occurrence of a specific event.

Contribution The excess of selling price over variable costs, from which fixed costs must be met, with any remaining contribution yielding profits. Its use emphasizes the importance of cost behavior patterns for decision-making.

Cost center A part of an organization for which costs are collected in detail, to be used for costing or control purposes.

Current assets Assets which circulate and change in the course of trading, usually within a period of a year. They include inventory, accounts receivable, prepayments and cash.

Current liabilities Those liabilities which have to be met in the short term, usually within one year.

Current ratio The ratio of current assets to current liabilities, used in assessing the adequacy of working capital and liquidity of an organization.

Debt/equity ratio A ratio (which can be calculated in a variety of ways) which identifies the relationship between debt and equity for a particular organization.

Decision tree A mapping out, in the form of a series of branches, of the various alternative courses of action which exist, so as to enable those alternatives to be better understood and the most efficient course of action to be chosen.

Depreciation The allocation of the acquisition cost of an asset to those periods or products which benefit from its use.

Differential costing A form of costing which relates to decisions about alternative courses of action, where only those factors which are different are considered.

Direct cost A cost which can be specifically identified with a particular product.

Direct labor hour rate A system of overhead absorption or recovery based upon the number of direct labor hours worked on particular products, units or jobs.

Discounted cash flow A system of adjusting for the time value of money such that cash flows at different times can be compared on an equal basis.

Efficiency variance The standard price for a particular resource, multiplied by the difference between the actual quantity of inputs used and the standard quantity allowed for the specific output.

Equity *See capital.*

Fixed assets Assets expected to confer benefit on an organization in the medium or long term. They include such things as land, buildings, plant, equipment, etc.

Fixed costs Costs which do not change as activity changes but which are essentially time based, e.g. rent and taxes, insurance, etc.

Fixed overhead volume variance The difference between hours actually worked and those budgeted, multiplied by the fixed overhead recovery rate per hour. This variance measures the amount of under- or over-recovery of fixed overhead due to a change in the capacity of the organization.

Fixed overhead spending variance The difference between actual and budgeted fixed overhead.

Flexible budget An overhead budget which is stated in terms of total fixed costs and variable costs per unit so that the total overhead may be calculated at different production volumes.

Funds flow statement A statement setting out the sources and uses of funds for a period.

Implicit budget A budget in which the person incurring costs has considerable freedom to set his own targets.

Indirect costs A cost which cannot be specifically identified with a particular product.

Internal rate of return *See yield.*

Inventory turnover The ratio of cost of goods sold to average inventory, used to measure the amount of inventory the firm is holding relative to its sales volume.

Job costing A system of recording costs of production in terms of each particular job, so that the cost of each job can be ascertained.

Labor The human effort involved in transforming materials into finished products.

Labor efficiency variance The difference between actual hours worked and the standard hours of actual production, multiplied by the standard labor rate. This gives the variance or difference in costs attributable to changes in labor efficiency.

Labor rate variance The difference between the actual rate of pay and the standard rate, multiplied by actual hours worked. This identifies the change in costs attributable to labor rate changes.

Liquid assets ratio The ratio of liquid assets to current liabilities, used to assess the adequacy of liquid funds of an organization.

Liquid funds Funds in a cash or near-cash form.

Machine hour rate A system of overhead absorption based upon the number of machine hours worked.

Margin of safety The excess of the current production level over the break-even level.

Marginal costing A system, sometimes referred to as variable costing, in which changes in variable costs are emphasized as being the relevant costs. These costs are deducted from revenues to give a contribution, from which fixed costs have to be met, any residual being profit.

Materials Those commodities used by a business in the production or trading process.

Materials price variance The difference between standard and actual cost, multiplied by actual usage, giving the variance attributable to changes in the price of materials.

Materials quantity variance The difference between actual materials used and the standard materials for actual production, multiplied by the standard cost. This gives the variance attributable to changes in the use of materials.

Net present value The difference between the present value of cash inflows and the present value of cash outflows, usually those associated with new capital projects.

Net present value per $1 of investment A system of ranking capital projects in a situation of limited funds, where the NPV is related to the amount of investment, so that the maximum return can be obtained from the funds available.

Opportunity cost The cost of foregoing a particular opportunity.

Overhead absorption (recovery) rate A rate which is added to direct costs of production, to provide an estimate of total production cost, by incorporating a share of overhead.

Overhead Costs incurred to facilitate the activity of the firm as a whole, which cannot be specifically identified with one particular product.

Participative budget A budget in which those subject to control and review have been closely involved.

Payback A system of evaluating capital projects based on the time it takes to recover the amount invested.

Performance appraisal The review of results with a view to ascertaining the efficiency of actual performance.

Price variance The difference between the actual price and the standard price of resources purchased, multiplied by the number of units purchased.

Prime cost The total of the direct costs of production.

Production cost The cost of production of output, including all factory overhead, but excluding other overhead.

Profit and loss statement A statement setting out the financial results of manufacturing and trading for a period.

Profit/volume graph A graph which relates the amount of profit to the level of production.

Relevant costs Costs which have a bearing on a particular decision to be made and need to be recognized in reaching a decision.

Return on assets The ratio of operating profit to operating assets, concerned with assessing the operating efficiency of an organization.

Return to ordinary shareholders The ratio of profit after tax and preferred dividends to ordinary shareholders equity, giving the percentage return being achieved by shareholders.

Risk preference The particular relationship between risk and expected returns which is preferred by an individual or organization.

Sales margin price variance The difference in selling price multiplied by actual sales, giving the variance attributable to changes in the selling price.

Sales margin quantity variance The difference in sales level (in units) multiplied by the standard margin per unit, giving the variance attributable to changes in the volume of sales.

Semi-variable costs Costs which contain both fixed and variable elements which change as production changes, but not directly in proportion to this change.

Sensitivity analysis An analysis of projects to ascertain how sensitive the final result is to changes in variables in the project.

Simulation A "pretend" run of a planned strategy with possible events being introduced (usually randomly) in an attempt to ascertain how successful the action is likely to be.

Standard costing A system of comparing actual results with expected results, the latter being based upon predetermined standard costs per unit. Under this system detailed variances can be calculated and analyzed, thus permitting the identification and control of particular problem areas.

Standard costs Predetermined costs per unit, usually broken down into considerable detail.

Time value of money The return which must be earned to compensate for postponing consumption (i.e. holding money) for a period, usually expressed as a rate of interest.

Total absorption costing The charging of overheads to units of production so as to ensure that all production overhead, as well as direct production costs, are effectively charged to such units, so that the production cost per unit of output can be calculated.

Unit costing A system of recording costs of production so as to arrive at a cost per unit of production.

Variable costs Costs which change in proportion to the level of activity.

Variable overhead efficiency variance The difference between actual hours worked and standard hours of actual production, multiplied by the standard variable overhead.

Variable overhead spending variance The difference between actual costs and actual hours, multiplied by the standard variable overhead.

Variance The difference between actual figures and expected figures, calculated so as to identify those areas in which actual performance is departing from planned performance, with a view to remedying this situation as soon as possible.

Working capital The amount of an organization's investment in short-term assets, less current liabilities.

Yield (or internal rate of return) The rate of return on a project at which the present value of inflows equals the present value of outflows.